Collins

MATHS FRAMEWORKING

Tiers 5–7

SATs Revision Guides

Complete Success for Mathematics at KS3

Name	Form	Date	Teacher

William Collins' dream of knowledge for all began with the publication of his first book in 1819. A self-educated mill worker, he not only enriched millions of lives, but also founded a flourishing publishing house. Today, staying true to this spirit, Collins books are packed with inspiration, innovation and practical expertise. They place you at the centre of a world of possibility and give you exactly what you need to explore it.

Collins. Do more.

Published by Collins
An imprint of HarperCollins*Publishers*
77–85 Fulham Palace Road
Hammersmith
London
W6 8JB

> Browse the complete Collins catalogue at
> **www.collinseducation.com**

ISBN 0 00 721162 7

Kevin Evans, Keith Gordon, Trevor Senior and Brian Speed assert their moral rights to be identified as the authors of this work

British Library Cataloguing in Publication Data.

A Catalogue record for this publication is available from the British Library

Commissioned by Marie Taylor
Project managed by Jenny Wong
Editorial support by Vicky Butt
Edited by Anita Clark
Proofread by Amanda Whyte
Design and typesetting by JPD
Covers by Chi Leung
Additional Illustration by Tony Wilkins
Production by Natasha Buckland

Printed and bound by Martins the Printers, Berwick-upon-Tweed

The publishers would like to thank the many teachers and advisers whose feedback helped to shape *Maths Frameworking*.

Every effort has been made to contact the holders of copyright material. But if any have been inadvertently overlooked, the Publishers will be pleased to make the necessary arrangements at the first opportunity.

Contents

How to use this book

Each double page covers one topic from the National Curriculum.
You will find the following features on each section.

Section title

This is the particular topic covered in the section.

Exercise number

This will help you find the answers at the back of the book.

Topic area

This is one of the four topic areas of the National Curriculum.

Level

This shows you the assessment level for the topic.

Marks per question

This will show you how to gain marks for your method.

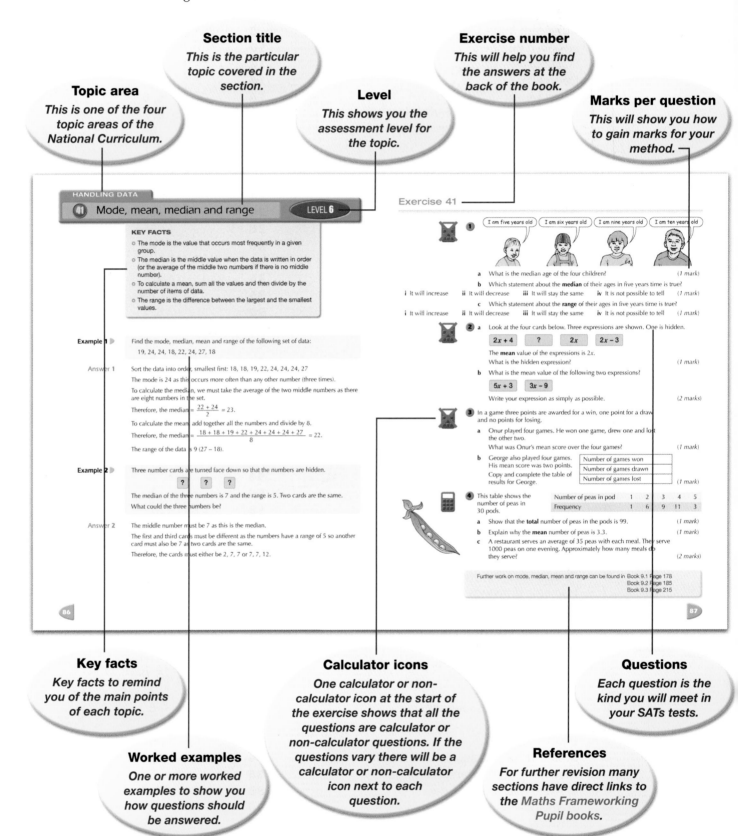

Key facts

Key facts to remind you of the main points of each topic.

Worked examples

One or more worked examples to show you how questions should be answered.

Calculator icons

One calculator or non-calculator icon at the start of the exercise shows that all the questions are calculator or non-calculator questions. If the questions vary there will be a calculator or non-calculator icon next to each question.

Questions

Each question is the kind you will meet in your SATs tests.

References

For further revision many sections have direct links to the Maths Frameworking Pupil books.

The National Curriculum tests or SATs

There are four tiers at which you can sit the tests:

- Tier 3–5
- Tier 4–6
- Tier 5–7
- Tier 6–8

Your teachers usually decide which tier you will be entered at. Make sure you know which one is your tier!

In each tier you take two written papers and a mental test.

- Paper 1 is a non-calculator paper.
- Paper 2 is a calculator paper.
- Mental test

Look for this icon.

All three papers have a total mark of 150. Usually you need about 90 marks in total to get the middle grade of each tier.

This book covers the written papers for tiers 5–7.

SATs topics

There are four Attainment Targets (ATs) in the National Curriculum:

- Number
- Algebra
- Shape, Space and Measures
- Handling Data

Each AT is divided into many different topics. These topics are covered in this book.

If there is a particular AT you have difficulty with, look it up in the contents page. You should work through all of the topics in that AT. If there are just a few topics you want extra help with, again use the contents page to find them.

On each section you will find a list of key facts and some worked examples. These may be enough to remind you of the main points of the topic. If you need more help, most sections have a reference to where you can find the topic in the *Maths Frameworking Pupil Books*.

SATs questions

In this book, all of the exercise questions will prepare you for your exams as they are in the style of the National Tests. The worked examples also show you typical questions and how they should be answered.

The number of marks for each question is shown. When you check your answers, you can see if you gained any part marks for showing correct methods. Always remember to show your working – you can still gain marks even if you do not get the correct answer.

Each topic shows the level at which it is assessed. If the topic covers more than one level, then the questions in the exercise will start with the lowest level and finish at the highest level.

Revision

Be sensible with revision.

Focus on what you are not sure about.

Don't leave it until the last minute.

If you don't understand something, ask your teacher.

If you use this book properly then you should gain the highest grade possible.

Best of luck with your tests!

KEY FACTS

- There are two common methods for multiplying three-digit by two-digit numbers: box method (partitioning) and column method.
- There are two common methods for dividing three-digit by two-digit numbers: subtracting multiples method and traditional method.

Example 1 ▷ One section of a football stadium holds 374 spectators. In total, the stadium has 26 sections of the same size. How many spectators does the stadium hold altogether?

Answer 1 If one section holds 374 spectators, the total number of spectators in 26 sections will be 374×26.

Use either the box method or column method to work out your answer.

Box method

	300	70	4	
20	6000	1400	80	7480
6	1800	420	24	2244
				9724

Column method

$$\begin{array}{r} 374 \\ 26 \\ \hline 2244 \ (6 \times 374) \\ 7480 \ (20 \times 374) \\ \hline 9724 \end{array}$$

The total number of spectators is 9724.

Example 2 ▷ 617 people go to the cinema to watch a film.

There are rows of seats inside the cinema. Each row has 23 seats.

What is the smallest number of rows needed if all 617 people are to watch the film?

Answer 2 To calculate the number of rows needed, you need to divide the number of people wanting to watch the film by the number of seats in each row: $617 \div 23$.

Use either the subtracting multiples method or traditional method to work out your answer.

Subtracting multiples method

$$\begin{array}{r} 617 \\ - \ 230 \ (10 \times 23) \\ \hline 387 \\ - \ 230 \ (10 \times 23) \\ \hline 157 \\ - \ 115 \ (5 \times 23) \\ \hline 42 \\ - \ 23 \ (1 \times 23) \\ \hline 19 \end{array}$$

Traditional method

$$\begin{array}{r} 26 \\ 23\overline{)617} \\ 46 \\ \hline 157 \\ 138 \\ \hline 19 \end{array}$$

The answer is 26 remainder 19. 26 rows will be full and 19 people will go onto another row. Therefore, 27 rows in total will be needed.

Exercise 1

1 Use any method to work out the following.

    a   27 × 32   *(1 mark)*

    b   342 × 65   *(2 marks)*

2 Use any method to work out the following.

    a   375 ÷ 21   *(2 marks)*

    b   723 ÷ 53   *(2 marks)*

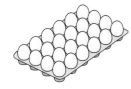

3 Eggs are delivered to shops on trays of 24.

    a   A shop orders 18 trays. How many eggs is this in total?   *(2 marks)*

    b   A different shop wants to order 300 eggs. How many full trays will need to be ordered so that the shop has at least 300 eggs?   *(2 marks)*

4 One bus holds 53 passengers.

    a   If they are all full, how many passengers can 35 buses carry?   *(2 marks)*

    b   A rugby club wants to transport 650 people to an away match. How many buses will they need to hire?   *(2 marks)*

5 Sets of books are sold in packs of 12.

    a   How many books will there be in 35 packs?   *(2 marks)*

    b   There are 250 students in a year group. If each student in the year group is to receive a book, how many packs will be needed?   *(2 marks)*

6 Tickets to a concert cost £18.00 each.

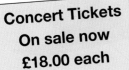

Concert Tickets
On sale now
£18.00 each

    a   220 people attend the concert. How much money is taken in ticket sales?   *(2 marks)*

    b   On a different day the ticket sales totalled £4500. How many people attended the concert on that day?   *(2 marks)*

Further work on multiplication and division can be found in

Book 8.1 Page 98, Book 9.1 Pages 207–11
Book 7.2 Page 98, Book 9.2 Pages 203–6
Book 7.3 Page 108

② Significant figures, approximation

LEVEL 7

KEY FACTS

- A number to one significant figure will have only one non-zero digit. Zeros in the number are used to show the correct place value: 70, 500, 0.008.
- A number to two significant figures will have two non-zero digits together: 17, 460, 12 000, 1.9.
- Round up or down depending upon the next number after the final significant digit: 5 or more round up; under 5 round down.

Example 1 ▷

The width of a tile is 400 mm, correct to the nearest millimetre.

a **i** What is the least possible width of one tile?

ii What is the greatest possible width of one tile?

b Five tiles are fixed to a wall to make a border. What is the least possible width of this border?

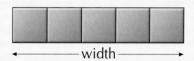
← width →

Answer 1

a **i** The smallest measure that could be rounded up to 400 mm is 399.5 mm.

ii The largest measure that could be rounded down to 400 mm is 400.4999 recurring mm. (The 'recurring' is important.)

b The smallest possible width of one tile is 399.5 mm. The minimum width of the border is therefore 5 × 399.5 = 1997.5 mm.

Example 2 ▷

A steam train used to run from Edinburgh to Kings Cross.

The train would travel at a steady 55 miles per hour and use 1 gallon of water for every 350 yards travelled.

Calculate how many gallons of water the train would have used in one hour of travelling. (There are 1760 yards in a mile.)

a Write down the full calculator display.

b Now write down your answer correct to two significant figures.

Answer 2

a In 1 hour the train would have travelled 55 miles. Find how many yards this is by multiplying 55 by 1760. Then divide this figure by the total number of yards travelled per gallon of water: 55 × 1760 ÷ 350 = 276.57143 gallons.

b 280 gallons

Exercise 2

1 The weight, to one significant figure, of one chocolate egg is 50 grams.

    a **i** What is the least possible weight of one chocolate egg?   *(1 mark)*

        ii What is the greatest possible weight of one chocolate egg?   *(1 mark)*

    b Billie buys eight chocolate eggs.

       What is the least possible total weight of Billie's eggs?   *(1 mark)*

2 The pie chart shows how people spend their earnings each month.

The sum of the percentages is not 100%.

Explain how this can happen if there is no mistake in the pie chart.

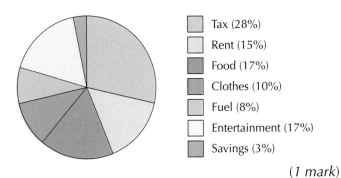

Tax (28%)
Rent (15%)
Food (17%)
Clothes (10%)
Fuel (8%)
Entertainment (17%)
Savings (3%)

   (1 mark)

3 Write down the approximate answers to one significant figure for the following problems.

Show your working.

    a $\dfrac{205 \times 487}{19}$ *(1 mark)*

    b $798 \times 107 \times 0.487$ *(1 mark)*

4 **a** Circle the best estimate of the answer to $83.7 \div 7.11$.

       8   9   10   11   12   13   *(1 mark)*

    b Circle the best estimate of the answer to 45.6×0.32.

       0   4.5   9   15   45   90   *(1 mark)*

    c Estimate the answer to $\dfrac{32.16 - 7.72}{2.93}$ giving your answer to 1 significant figure.   *(1 mark)*

    d Estimate the answer to $\dfrac{31.7 \times 18.9}{8.68 \times 5.83}$.   *(1 mark)*

5 **a** Use your calculator to work out

$$\frac{6.7 + \sqrt{6.7^2 - 4 \times 1.2 \times 5.6}}{2 \times 1.2}$$

       Show all the digits in your calculator display.   *(1 mark)*

    b Write your answer to 2 significant figures.   *(1 mark)*

Further work on rounding and significant figures can be found in Book 9.1 Page 104
Book 9.2 Pages 32, 105
Book 9.3 Pages 37, 126

3 Negative numbers

KEY FACTS

- Negative numbers are also called directed numbers.
- When answering questions involving negative numbers, it is useful to draw a number line if there isn't one in the question.

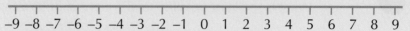

$$-9\ -8\ -7\ -6\ -5\ -4\ -3\ -2\ -1\ \ 0\ \ 1\ \ 2\ \ 3\ \ 4\ \ 5\ \ 6\ \ 7\ \ 8\ \ 9$$

- Always start counting at zero on a number line.
- Negative numbers move to the left or down and positive numbers move to the right or up.
- Two signs the same together (+ + or – –) are equivalent to a single plus: $+4 - -5 = +9$, $-3 + +6 = +3$
- Two different signs together (+ – or – +) are equivalent to a single minus: $-3 - +6 = -9$, $+5 + -6 = -1$
- Multiplying or dividing two positive numbers or two negative numbers gives a positive answer: $-2 \times -3 = +6$, $-3 \div -2 = +1.5$
- Multiplying or dividing two numbers with different signs gives a negative answer: $-4 \times +3 = -12$, $+6 \div -2 = -3$

Example 1 ▷

Look at the following list of numbers: –8, –6, –3, –1, 3, 6, 8, 9

a What is the total of all eight numbers in the list?

b Choose the three numbers from the list which have the lowest possible total. Do not use the same number more than once.

c Choose three numbers from the list to make the following calculation true:
$$... + ... + ... = 0$$

Answer 1

a The total is 8 (or +8).
The calculation can be made easier by grouping numbers together so they cancel each other out: $(-8 + 8) + (-6 + -3 + 9) + -1 + 3 + 6 = 8$

b The smallest total is given by adding the three smallest numbers which are the three negative numbers –8, –6 and –3. Therefore: $-8 + -6 + -3 = -17$

c There are two possible answers: $-6 + -3 + 9 = 0$ or $-8 + -1 + 9 = 0$

Exercise 3

1 The chart shows the range in temperature (minimum to maximum) in December 2004 for a number of cities in Europe.

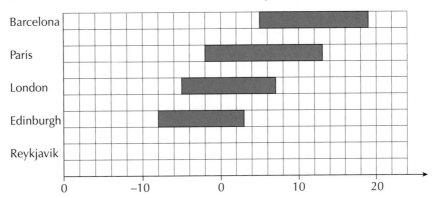

a What was the **minimum** temperature in London? *(1 mark)*

b What was the range of temperature in Edinburgh? *(1 mark)*

c In Reykjavik the minimum temperature was −16°C and the range of temperature was 12°C. Draw the bar to show this information. *(1 mark)*

2 a A number machine maps the number n to the number $n - 5$.
Fill in the missing values.

n	→	$n - 5$
2	→	...
...	→	−20

(2 marks)

b A number machine maps the number n to the number $-5n$.
Fill in the missing values.

n	→	$-5n$
2	→	...
...	→	+20

(2 marks)

3 Fill in the blank boxes using only negative numbers to give the value 20.

a $\square \times \square = 20$ **b** $\square - \square = 20$ *(2 marks)*

4 a Two numbers **multiply** together to make −12 and they **add** together to make 1. What are the two numbers? *(2 marks)*

b Two numbers **multiply** together to make +12 and **add** together to make −8. What are the two numbers? *(2 marks)*

c 6 squared is 36. The square of another number is also 36. What is the other number? *(1 mark)*

5 Work out the following.

a $+7 - +9 = \ldots\ldots$ **b** $-8 - +7 = \ldots\ldots$ **c** $-5 + -3 = \ldots\ldots$

d $+2 \times -8 = \ldots\ldots$ **e** $-24 \div -3 = \ldots\ldots$ **f** $+8 + -6 \times +3 = \ldots\ldots$ *(6 marks)*

Further work on negative numbers can be found in Book 8.1 Page 2
Book 8.2 Page 2
Book 8.3 Page 2

4 Fractions

KEY FACTS

o Fractions can only be added or subtracted if they have the same denominator. If you are asked to add or subtract fractions with different denominators, you must find the lowest common denominator:

$$\frac{2}{3} + \frac{1}{5} = \frac{10}{15} + \frac{3}{15} = \frac{13}{15}, \frac{3}{4} - \frac{2}{5} = \frac{15}{20} - \frac{8}{20} = \frac{7}{20}$$

o When multiplying fractions, cancel by any common factors top and bottom before multiplying the numerators and denominators.

$$\frac{3}{4} \times \frac{2}{9} = \frac{\overset{1}{\cancel{3}}}{\cancel{4}_2} \times \frac{\overset{1}{\cancel{2}}}{\cancel{9}_3} = \frac{1}{6}$$

o When dividing by a fraction, turn it upside down and multiply by it.

$$\frac{2}{9} \div \frac{1}{3} = \frac{2}{\cancel{9}_3} \times \frac{\overset{1}{\cancel{3}}}{1} = \frac{2}{3}$$

o When adding and subtracting mixed numbers, separate the whole numbers and the fractions and deal with them separately.

o When multiplying and dividing mixed numbers make them into top heavy fractions first.

Example 1 ▷

a   A farmer is selling a field for building.

Company A buys $\frac{1}{10}$ of the field.
Company B buys $\frac{1}{4}$ of the field.
Company C buys $\frac{2}{5}$ of the field.
Company D buys the rest of the field.
What fraction of the field does company D buy?

b   Another farmer is selling a field for building divided into 20 equal plots.
One plot costs £20 000.
A company buys $\frac{3}{5}$ of the plots.
How much do they pay?

Answer 1

a   Between them companies A, B and C buy $\frac{1}{10} + \frac{1}{4} + \frac{2}{5}$ of the field.

You need to add these fractions together, so first find the lowest common denominator of 10, 4 and 5: 20.

Next, change all the fractions into twentieths: $\frac{1}{10} + \frac{1}{4} + \frac{2}{5} = \frac{2}{20} + \frac{5}{20} + \frac{8}{20}$

And then add the numerators: $= \frac{15}{20}$

The whole field is equal to 1, so subtract the total from 1: $1 - \frac{15}{20} = \frac{5}{20}$

Finally, answer the question, simplifying your answer:
Company D buys $\frac{5}{20} = \frac{1}{4}$ of the field.

b $\frac{3}{5}$ of 20 plots $= \frac{3}{5} \times 20 = \frac{3}{5} \times \frac{20}{1} = 12$

12 plots cost 12 × £20 000 = £240 000

Exercise 4

1 The table shows some fractions of amounts of money.

Use the table to help you work out the missing numbers.

	£6	£12	£22
$\frac{1}{2}$	£3.00	£6.00	£11.00
$\frac{1}{4}$	£1.50	£3.00	£5.50
$\frac{1}{8}$	£0.75	£1.50	£2.25

a $\frac{3}{4}$ of £22 = ...

b £4.50 = $\frac{3}{8}$ of ......

c £3.75 = ... of £6

d £0.75 = $\frac{1}{16}$ of ...... *(4 marks)*

2 Fill in the missing numbers or fractions.

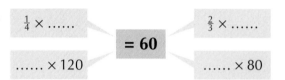

$\frac{1}{4} \times$ ......

$\frac{2}{3} \times$ ......

= 60

...... $\times 120$

...... $\times 80$ *(4 marks)*

3 a Mark the following fractions on the number line: $\frac{1}{4}$ $\frac{7}{12}$ $\frac{2}{3}$

0     $\frac{1}{2}$ 1 *(3 marks)*

b Fill in the missing numbers.

$\frac{3}{12} = \frac{\square}{4}$ $\qquad$ $\frac{3}{4} = \frac{12}{\square}$ $\qquad$ $\frac{1}{\square} = \frac{8}{40}$ *(3 marks)*

4 a How many **fifths** are there in $2\frac{2}{5}$? *(1 mark)*

b Work out $2\frac{2}{5} \div \frac{3}{5}$. *(2 marks)*

5 a Work out the area of this triangle. *(3 marks)*

b How many of these triangles will fit into a rectangle that is 4 cm by 10 cm? *(2 marks)*

$\frac{4}{5}$ cm

$3\frac{1}{3}$ cm

6 Work out the following.

a $\frac{4}{5} - \frac{1}{4}$ $\qquad$ b $2\frac{3}{8} + 1\frac{2}{3}$ $\qquad$ c $1\frac{3}{5} \times \frac{15}{16}$ $\qquad$ d $2\frac{2}{9} \div 1\frac{2}{3}$ *(4 marks)*

7 The fraction $\frac{3}{8}$ is halfway between $\frac{1}{4}$ and $\frac{1}{2}$.

What fraction is halfway between the following?

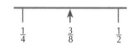

$\frac{1}{4}$ $\qquad$ $\frac{3}{8}$ $\qquad$ $\frac{1}{2}$

a $\frac{1}{8}$ and $\frac{1}{4}$ $\qquad\qquad$ b $\frac{1}{3}$ and $\frac{5}{6}$ *(2 marks)*

8 Put the following fractions in order, with the smallest first. Show your method clearly.

$\frac{3}{8}$ $\qquad$ $\frac{5}{16}$ $\qquad$ $\frac{2}{7}$ $\qquad$ $\frac{1}{3}$ *(2 marks)*

Further work on fractions can be found in Book 9.1 Pages 21–26, 162
Book 9.2 Pages 16, 18, 169
Book 9.3 Pages 18, 197

5 Decimals

KEY FACTS

- To multiply a decimal by 10 or 100, move the digits one or two places to the left, using zero place holders as required.
- To divide a decimal by 10 or 100, move the digits one or two places to the right, using zero place holders as required.
- To add or subtract decimals, line up the decimal point and add extra zeros if required.
- To multiply or divide decimals by a whole number, keep the same number of decimal places in the answer as in the question.

Example 1

a 3.24×10 **b** 27.6×100 **c** $82.4 \div 10$ **d** $5.87 \div 100$

Answer 1

a $3.24 \times 10 = 32.4$ **b** $27.6 \times 100 = 2760$

c $82.4 \div 10 = 8.24$ **d** $5.87 \div 100 = 0.0587$

$$3.24 \rightarrow 32.4$$

$$27.6 \rightarrow 2760$$

$$82.4 \rightarrow 8.24$$

$$5.87 \rightarrow 0.0587$$

Example 2

a $3.2 + 5.97$ **b** $39.34 - 17.8$ **c** 7.36×7 **d** $8.76 \div 4$

Answer 2

a
```
   3.20
 + 5.97
   9.17
     1
```

b
```
  8 1
 39.34
-17.80
 21.54
```

c
```
   7.36
 ×    7
  51.52
   2 4
```

d
```
   2.19
4)8.7³6
```

Example 3

Phil pays £24.80 in bus fares each week to travel to work.

a How much does he pay for 4 weeks?

b How much does he save if he buys a monthly bus pass for £72.50?

Answer 3

a Write the calculation in columns
```
   24.80
 ×     4
   99.20
    1 3
```

b Write the calculation in columns
```
  8 1
 99.20
-72.50
 26.70
```

Exercise 5

1 Work out the following.

    a 6.72×10 **b** 0.256×100 **c** $54.3 \div 10$ **d** $90.4 \div 100$ *(4 marks)*

2 Fill in the missing numbers.

    a $7.2 \times \boxed{} = 72$ **b** $\boxed{} \times 100 = 82.4$

    c $742.3 \div \boxed{} = 7.423$ **d** $\boxed{} \div 10 = 0.489$ *(4 marks)*

3 Work out the following.

    a $2.56 + 3.48$ **b** $8.7 + 24.65$ **c** $9.62 - 5.38$ **d** $8 - 2.36$ *(4 marks)*

4 Work out the following.

    a 4.27×5 **b** 3.63×9 **c** $82.5 \div 5$ **d** $37.04 \div 8$ *(4 marks)*

5 Steve has these number cards. 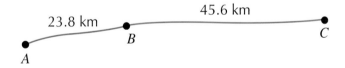

    He makes the number 3.52 with four of the cards.

    a Use the cards to make a number 10 times as big as 3.52   *(1 mark)*

    b Use the cards to make a number 100 times as big as 3.52   *(1 mark)*

6 Copy and complete this school order.

100 blue biros at £0.22 each	£......
100 pencils at £0.12 each	£......
100 rubbers at £0.08 each	£......
Total £	

    (3 marks)

7 The diagram shows the distances between three towns *A*, *B* and *C*.

    23.8 km   45.6 km

    A   *B*   *C*

    a How far is it from *A* to *C*?   *(1 mark)*

    b How much shorter is the distance from *A* to *B* than from *B* to *C*?   *(1 mark)*

8 Rebecca buys three CDs at £8.75 each and four DVDs at £12.99 each.
How much does she pay altogether?   *(3 marks)*

9 A lottery syndicate of six people wins £436.80.
If they share it out equally, how much does each person receive?   *(1 mark)*

10 Which is the larger amount: one fifth of £48 or one eighth of £74?   *(2 marks)*

Further work on decimals can be found in Book 7.1 Pages 13, 164
Book 7.2 Pages 13, 161
Book 7.3 Page 14

KEY FACTS

- Percentage is a way of representing a number as a fraction of 100. Therefore, 1% represents 1 out of 100, 100% means everything and 50% means half.
- To find N% of M calculate N × M ÷ 100.
- Change a fraction to a percentage by multiplying it by 100.
- Change a decimal to a percentage by multiplying it by 100.

Example 1 ▷ Joy asked 60 children which colour they liked best.

a Which colour did 50% of the boys like best?

b Which colour did 15% of the girls like best?

c Joy said: "In my survey, green was just as popular with boys as with girls." Explain why Joy was wrong.

Colour	Number of boys	Number of girls
Blue	10	13
Red	3	9
Yellow	5	10
Pink	0	6
Green	2	2
	20	**40**

d Which colour was equally popular with boys and girls?

Answer 1 **a** 50% is a half. There are 20 boys in total so half of 20 is 10 boys. Blue is the colour that 10 boys said they liked best. So 50% of the boys liked blue best.

b There are 40 girls in total. 10% of 40 is 4, 5% of 40 is 2, so 15% of 40 is 4 + 2 = 6. Pink is the colour that six girls liked best. So 15% of the girls liked pink best.

c Although an equal number of boys and girls said they liked green best, the percentage of boys choosing green is different to the percentage of girls choosing green. The two boys who liked green represent 2 out of 20 which is 10% of the boys. The two girls who liked green represent 2 out of 40 which is 5% of the girls.

d Yellow is equally popular with boys and girls. This can be seen from the table since the fraction of boys choosing yellow is $\frac{5}{20}$, equal to $\frac{1}{4}$ which is 25%. The fraction of girls is $\frac{10}{40}$, also $\frac{1}{4}$ and 25%.

Example 2 ▷ Calculate the missing numbers.

a 15% of £60 = £☐

b 15% of £☐ = £6

c ☐% of £80 = £16

Answer 2 **a** 15% of £60 = 15 × 60 ÷ 100 = £9.

b If 15% represents £6, then 5% (15% ÷ 3) represents £2 (£6 ÷ 3).
So 10% (5% × 2) represents £4 (£2 × 2).

So 100% (10% × 10) represents £40 (£4 × 10).

Hence 15% of **£40** = £6.

c   The question is really asking: "What percentage of £80 is £16?"

In other words, what percentage is the fraction $\frac{16}{80}$.

This is found by multiplying the fraction by 100.

So, 16 ÷ 80 × 100 = 20%.

Exercise 6

1   The table shows some percentages of amounts of money.

Use the table to work out the missing numbers.

	£10	£70	£105
5%	50p	£3.50	£5.25
10%	£1	£7	£10.50

a   15% of £70 = £ ☐   (1 mark)

b   £7.50 = ☐ % of £10   (1 mark)

c   £1.75 = 5% of £ ☐   (1 mark)

2   The table shows the 2004 population of each of the world's continents.

a   Which continent had approximately 8% of the world's population in 2004?   (1 mark)

b   In 2004, what percentage of the world's population was living in Asia?   (2 marks)

Continent	Population (in millions)
Australia	31
Africa	823
Antarctica	0
Asia	3737
Europe	729
North America	486
South America	351
World total	**6157**

3   A report on the number of MPs in the UK in 2004 found: "There are 659 MPs. About 18% of them are women."

a   The percentage was rounded to the nearest whole number, 18.

Which of the numbers below is the smallest value the percentage could have been, to one decimal place?

17.1%	17.2%	17.3%	17.4%	17.5%
17.6%	17.7%	17.8%	17.9%	18.0%

(1 mark)

b   What is the smallest number of women MPs that there might have been in 2004? (Use your answer to part **a** to help you calculate this answer.)   (2 marks)

Further work on percentages can be found in   Book 8.1 Page 45
                                              Book 8.2 Page 47
                                              Book 8.3 Page 54

7 Percentage and proportional change

KEY FACTS

○ When a value, V, is increased or decreased by a percentage, P, the formula is:

$$\text{New value} = V(1 \pm \frac{P}{100})$$

○ The quantity $1 \pm \frac{P}{100}$ is called a multiplier and is useful when calculating with percentages.

○ To work out a proportional change, calculate the value of one item. For example, if seven books cost £41.79, what is the cost of 12 books?

Calculate the cost of one book: £41.79 ÷ 7 = £5.97.

Now calculate the cost of 12 books: 12 × £5.97 = £71.64.

This is called the Unitary Method.

Example 1 ▷ 1 kilogram (1 kg) ≈ 2.2 pound weight (2.2 lb). 1 pound weight (1 lb) = 16 ounces (16 oz).

   a   How many ounces is 5 kg?   **b**   How many grams is 1 lb?

Answer 1   **a**   5 kg = 5 × 2.2 lb = 11 lb

               11 lb = 11 × 16 oz = 176 oz

    b   1 lb = 1 kg ÷ 2.2

               1 kg = 1000 g

               1000 g ÷ 2.2 ≈ 455 g

Example 2 ▷ In 1996, 81 755 400 passengers travelled by air in and out of the UK.

In 2002, 105 677 600 passengers travelled by air in and out of the UK.

Calculate the percentage increase in air passengers in the UK between 1996 and 2002.

Answer 2   The actual increase is 105677600 − 81755400 = 23922200.

The percentage increase is $\frac{23922200}{81755400} \times 100 = 29.26\%$.

Exercise 7

1 **a**   A standard pack of dishwasher powder contains 1 kg of powder.

      The recommended amount for one wash is 40 g of powder.

      How many washes can you get from one packet of powder?   *(1 mark)*

   b   A special offer pack contains 20% more powder than a standard pack.

      How many washes can you get from a special offer pack?   *(1 mark)*

2 Winston's journey to work is normally 18 miles.

   a A road diversion increases the distance by 35%. How far is this journey? *(2 marks)*

   b On the way home Winston takes another route which is 4 miles longer than his normal route. What percentage of 18 miles is 4 miles? *(2 marks)*

3 £1 = $1.80 (US dollars). £1 = €2.40 (Euros).

   a How much is £2.55 in US dollars? *(1 mark)*

   b How much is €4.50 in pounds? *(1 mark)*

   c How many Euros will you get for $558 (US dollars)? *(2 marks)*

4 The cost of a Breezyjet Airlines flight depends on how soon before you intend to fly you book a ticket.

Time of booking	Percentage of full fare
Within 1 week	100%
1–2 weeks	85%
2 weeks–1 month	65%
1–2 months	50%
2–3 months	40%
Over 3 months	30%

   a A Breezyjet flight from Luton to Nice has a full fare of £160. How much will the fare be if you book 2 months 2 weeks before the flight time? *(2 marks)*

   b A Breezyjet flight from Liverpool to Dublin has a full fare of £68. John pays £44.20. When did he book the flight? *(2 marks)*

5 **a** In 1975 the price of a VW beetle car was £1440 and sales tax was charged at 15%. How much tax would a customer have paid? *(2 marks)*

   b In 2005 the price of a VW beetle is £10 682 including sales tax of £1282. What percentage of the price is tax? *(2 marks)*

6 **a** Which of these calculations gives the answer to the question: What is 14% of £56?

   14×56 0.14×56 1.14×56 1.4×56 *(1 mark)*

   b Which of these gives the answer to the question: What is 14 increased by 56%?

   56×14 0.56×14 1.56×14 5.6×14 *(1 mark)*

   c Fill in the missing value.
   To increase a quantity by 15% multiply by … *(1 mark)*

7 In 1901 the population of Leeds was 552 479. In 2001 it was 715 404. What is the percentage increase in the population of Leeds between 1901 and 2001? *(2 marks)*

Further work on proportional change can be found in Book 9.1 Page 29
Book 9.2 Page 21
Book 9.3 Page 21

8 Ratio

KEY FACTS

- Ratios are simplified by cancelling by the highest common factor in the same way as cancelling fractions.
  For example, £10 : £15 = 2 : 3 (divide both numbers by 5).
  Note that there are no units in the answer.
- Ratios are often written in the form 1 : n.
  For example, 4 : 9 = 1 : 2.25 (divide both numbers by 4).
- When dividing a quantity in a given ratio, first add up the total number of parts, then work out what one part is worth and finally multiply this amount by each of the ratios.

Example 1 ▷ A drink is made from orange juice and lemonade in the ratio 2 : 5.
How much lemonade is needed if 100 ml of orange juice is used?

Answer 1 The ratio of orange juice to lemonade must cancel down to 2 : 5.
100 : x = 2 : 5, so each number needs to be multiplied by 50 to give x = 5 × 50 = 250.
250 ml of lemonade is needed.

Example 2 ▷ Anne and Dave divide £40 between them in the ratio 3 : 5.
How much does each person receive?

Answer 2 The ratio 3 : 5 means that there are 3 + 5 = 8 equal parts.
So 1 part = £40 ÷ 8 = £5.
Anne receives £5 × 3 = £15 and Dave receives £5 × 5 = £25.

Exercise 8

1 Write each of the following ratios in its simplest form.

    a 4 : 12   **b** 9 : 15   **c** 14 : 49   **d** 36 : 48   *(4 marks)*

2 Write each of the following ratios in the form 1: n.

    a 2 : 7   **b** 4 : 10   **c** 5 : 8   **d** 10 : 27   *(4 marks)*

3 The ratio of the weights of the two cereal packets is 2 : 3.
Find the weight in the larger packet.   *(2 marks)*

4 **a** In Andy's class, there are 14 boys and 16 girls.
Write down the ratio of boys to girls in its simplest form.   *(1 mark)*

    b In Joan's class the ratio of boys to girls is 4 : 5.
How many boys are in the class, if there are 15 girls?   *(1 mark)*

5 **a** Divide £80 in the ratio 1 : 4. *(2 marks)*

b Divide 120 kg in the ratio 3 : 7. *(2 marks)*

6 Copy and shade the diagram so that the ratio of shaded squares to unshaded squares is 3 : 5.

(2 marks)

7 In a wood there are oak trees, beech trees and sycamore trees in the ratio 1 : 2 : 3.
Find the number of each type of tree if there are 600 trees in the wood. *(2 marks)*

8 As a Christmas present, Grandma Wilson decides to share out £60 between her two grandchildren in the ratio of their ages.

a How much does each child receive, if Hannah is 4 years old and Jack is 6 years old? *(2 marks)*

b The following Christmas she shares out £60 again in the ratio of their ages.
How much does each child receive on the following Christmas? *(2 marks)*

9 The design below is made from two grey squares and one black square.

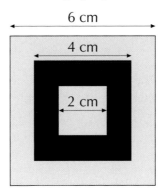

Find the ratio of the black area to the grey area, giving your answer in its simplest form. *(3 marks)*

10 A supermarket sells tins of baked beans in two sizes.
The small tin costs 25p and the large tin costs 40p.

a Write down the ratio of the weights of the two tins in its simplest form. *(1 mark)*

b Write down the ratio of the cost of the two tins in its simplest form. *(1 mark)*

c Which tin gives the better value for money? *(2 marks)*

Further work on ratio can be found in Book 8.3 Page 189
Book 9.1 Page 27
Book 9.2 Page 26

9 Powers and roots

LEVEL **6, 7**

KEY FACTS

- $3^4 = 3 \times 3 \times 3 \times 3 = 81$. (3 is the base number and 4 is the power or index.)

  On a calculator use the $\boxed{y^x}$ key.

- Laws of indices: $x^a \times x^b = x^{a+b}$

  $\qquad\qquad\qquad x^a \div x^b = x^{a-b}$

  $\qquad\qquad\qquad (x^a)^b = x^{ab}$

- $\sqrt{25} = 5$ or -5, because $5 \times 5 = 25$ or $-5 \times -5 = 25$. This is written as ± 5.

  On a calculator use the $\boxed{\sqrt{x}}$ key.

- $\sqrt[3]{27} = 3$, because $3 \times 3 \times 3 = 27$.

  On a calculator use the $\boxed{\sqrt[3]{x}}$ key.

Example 1 ▷ Which is the bigger number, 4^5 or 5^4?

Answer 1 $\quad 4^5 = 1024$ and $5^4 = 625$, so 4^5 is the bigger number.

Example 2 ▷ Solve the equation $x^2 = 85$.

Answer 2 $\quad x = \sqrt{85}$, so $x = 9.2$ or $x = -9.2$ (1dp).

Exercise 9

1 Work out the following.

    a 2^7 **b** 3^6 **c** 10^8 (*3 marks*)

2 Work out the following, leaving your answer in index form.

    a $4^3 \times 4^5$ **b** $5^8 \div 5^2$ **c** $(7^3)^4$ (*3 marks*)

3 Solve the following equations.

    a $x^2 = 16$ **b** $x^2 - 7 = 93$ **c** $2x^2 + 8 = 26$ (*6 marks*)

4 Solve the following equations.

    a $x^3 = 64$ **b** $x^3 - 1 = 26$ **c** $4x^3 - 10 = 22$ (*3 marks*)

5 Here are some number cards.

$$2^5 \quad 3^4 \quad 4^3 \quad 5^2 \quad 6^1$$

    a Which number is the largest? *(2 marks)*

    b Which number is equal to 8^2? *(1 mark)*

6 **a** Find the values of a and b.
$625 = 25^a = 5^b$ *(2 marks)*

    b Find the values of m and n.
$2^m \times 3^n = 72$ *(2 marks)*

7 For each of these cards n can be any positive number.

$$2n \quad \frac{1}{2} \quad \frac{n}{2} \quad n^2 \quad \sqrt{n}$$

    a Which card will always give an answer greater than n? *(1 mark)*

    b When $n = 1$, which cards will also give the answer 1? *(2 marks)*

    c When $n = 2.4$, which cards will give an answer less than 2.4? *(2 marks)*

8 Some numbers are greater than their squares.
For example: $0.5 > 0.5^2$
Which numbers are equal to their squares? *(2 marks)*

9 $\sqrt{12}$ lies between 3 and 4, since $3^2 = 9$ and $4^2 = 16$.
Find two consecutive whole numbers that each of the following lies between:

    a $\sqrt{40}$ **b** $\sqrt{90}$ **c** $\sqrt{200}$ *(3 marks)*

10 The square on the right has an area of 42 cm^2.
Find the side length, l, giving your answer
to one decimal place.

(1 mark)

11 This cube has a volume of 100 m^3.
Find the length of each side, s, giving
your answer to one decimal place. *(1 mark)*

12 **a** Substitute different values for x and y to show that
$\sqrt{x} \times \sqrt{y} = \sqrt{xy}$ *(2 marks)*

    b Substitute different values for x and y to show that
$\sqrt{x} + \sqrt{y} \neq \sqrt{x + y}$ *(2 marks)*

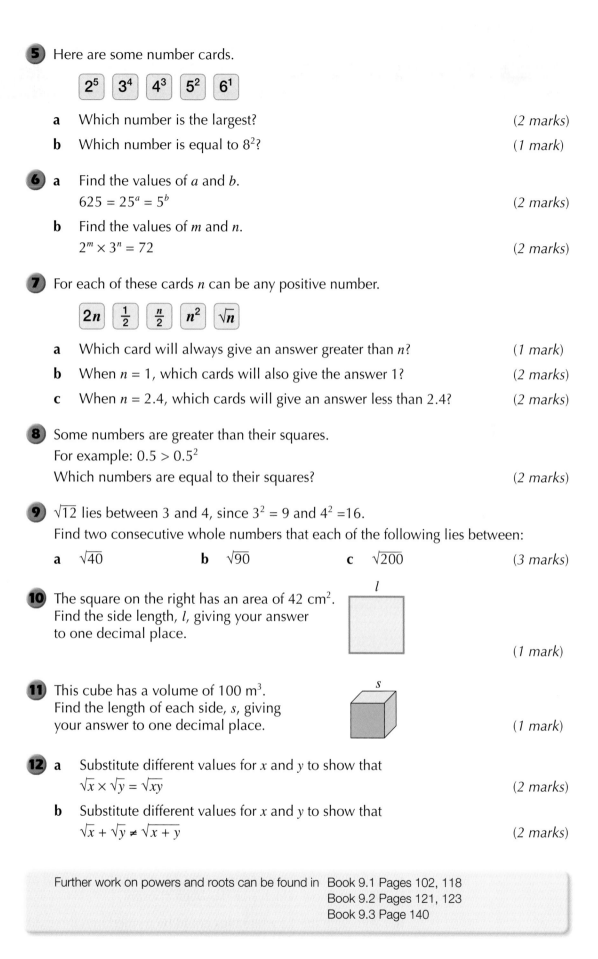

Further work on powers and roots can be found in   Book 9.1 Pages 102, 118
                                           Book 9.2 Pages 121, 123
                                           Book 9.3 Page 140

KEY FACTS

○ Each number in a sequence is called a term.

○ Each term has a position in the sequence. For example, 1st, 2nd, 3rd, 4th.

○ The value of a term can be found by using its position in the sequence. For example, the nth term in the sequence 1, 2, 3, 4, … is n; the nth term in 3, 6, 9, 12, … is $3n$; the nth term in 1, 4, 9, 16, … is n^2.

○ Sequences can be described by a 'term-to-term' rule or by an algebraic rule (nth term).

○ If a sequence increases by the same value each time, the nth term will be of the form $an + b$, where a is the constant incremental value. For example, the sequence 3, 7, 11, 15, … increases by 4 each time. The nth term is $4n + b$, to find b add or subtract to get the first term, so $4 - 1 = 3$, giving $b = -1$.

○ Two special sequences are the square numbers (1, 4, 9, 16, 25, 36, …) and the triangle numbers (1, 3, 6, 10, 15, 21, …).

Example 1 ▷ Trevor is making rectangular patterns with black, grey and white square tiles. He uses black tiles for the corners, grey tiles for the edges and white tiles for the middle.

a Complete the table to show how many tiles of each colour are used in a 4 by 6 rectangle.

b Trevor makes a rectangle using five white tiles for the middle. How many grey tiles will the rectangle have?

c Trevor now makes a rectangle using 24 white tiles for the middle. Explain why you cannot say how many grey tiles the rectangle will have.

Colour	Number
Black	
Grey	
White	
Total	24

d Trevor has four black tiles, 14 grey tiles and 12 white tiles. If he uses **all** of the tiles there is only one rectangle that he can make. Draw the rectangle.

Answer 1   **a** There are four black tiles, 12 grey tiles and eight white tiles. Check that these total 24: $4 + 12 + 8 = 24$.

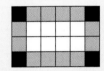

b As 5 is a prime number it can only be arranged in a 1 by 5 rectangle.

There will be 12 grey tiles.

c As 24 can be arranged in a 1 by 24, a 2 by 12, a 3 by 8 and a 4 by 6 rectangle you do not know which size has been chosen.

d Although the 12 white tiles could be formed into three different middles (1 by 12, 2 by 6 or 3 by 4) there is only one middle (3 by 4) that uses 14 grey tiles.

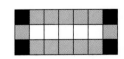

Exercise 10

1 The table shows the counting numbers arranged in a five-column grid.

	Col 1	Col 2	Col 3	Col 4	Col 5
Row 1	1	2	3	4	5
Row 2	⑥	7	8	9	10
Row 3	11	⑫	13	14	15
Row 4	16	17	⑱	19	20
Row 5	21	22	23	㉔	25
Row 6					

  a   Which column will the number 78 be in?   *(1 mark)*

  b   Column 1 forms the sequence 1, 6, 11, 16, 21, ...
What number in this sequence will be in the tenth row?   *(1 mark)*

  c   The nth term of the numbers in the fourth column is $5n - 1$.
What is the nth term of the numbers in column 3?   *(1 mark)*

  d   The numbers in the 6 times table are shown circled.
Row 1 does not contain any numbers in the 6 times table.
Which is the next row that does not contain any numbers in the
6 times table?   *(1 mark)*

2 The nth term of a sequence is given by the rule: 'Square the number n and add 1'.
For $n = 1, 2, 3, 4, ...$ this generates the sequence: 2, 5, 10, 17, ...

  a   Work out the value of the 100th term of the sequence.   *(1 mark)*

  b   Write down an expression for the nth term of the sequence.   *(1 mark)*

  c   Use this expression to help you find how many numbers in the
sequence are less than 900.   *(1 mark)*

3 Hexagons can be made from matches.

 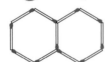  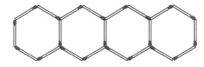

1 hexagon	2 hexagon	3 hexagon	4 hexagon
6 matches	11 matches	16 matches	21 matches

Which of the following expressions shows the number of matches, M,
needed for H hexagons?

$$H = 6M \qquad H = 6M + 5 \qquad H = 5M + 1 \qquad H = 5M - 1 \qquad \text{\textit{(1 mark)}}$$

4 The pyramid of numbers below is built up row by row.

```
            1                    Row 1
        2   3   4                Row 2
      5  6  7  8  9              Row 3
   10 11 12 13 14 15 16          Row 4
```

  a   An expression for the middle number in row n is $n^2 - n + 1$.
Write an expression for each of the following:
   i   the number on the right side of the middle number   *(1 mark)*
   ii   the number on the left side of the middle number.   *(1 mark)*

  b   Calculate the middle number in row 12.   *(1 mark)*

  c   Write an expression for the last number in row n.   *(1 mark)*

Further work on number patterns and generalisation can be found in   Book 9.1 Pages 2–10
Book 9.2 Pages 2, 5, 13
Book 9.3 Pages 2, 5, 46

Expressions, formulae and equations

KEY FACTS

○ Like terms are ones that contain the same letter (and power). So $3q$, $8q$, $-2q$ and q are all like terms.

○ Like terms can easily be added or subtracted using their coefficients. For example: $3a + 5a = 8a$, $9q - 4q = 5q$.

○ Unlike terms cannot be simplified. For example: $2x + 3y$.

○ When expanding a single bracket the number or letter outside has to multiply everything inside. For example:
$2(x - 4) = 2 \times x - 2 \times 4 = 2x - 8$, $z(z + 5) = z \times z + z \times 5 = z^2 + 5z$

Example 1 ▷ Look at the table opposite.

	Number of CDs
Alan	a
Bahvna	b

Write in words the meaning of each equation.

The first one has been done for you.

$a = 14$	Alan has 14 CDs
$a + b = 56$	
$b = 3a$	

Answer 1
a $a + b = 56$ means Alan and Bahvna have 56 CDs between them.

b $b = 3a$ means Bahvna has three times as many CDs as Alan.

Example 2 ▷ Wesley has a pile of cards. An expression for the **total** number of cards is $6n + 9$.

a Wesley puts the cards in two piles.

The number of cards in one pile is $4n + 5$.

Write an expression to show the number of cards in the pile of cards on the left.

b Wesley puts all the cards together. Then he uses them to make three equal piles.

Write an expression to show the number of cards in one of the piles.

c Wesley puts all the cards together again and uses them to make two different piles.

There are 11 cards in the left pile.

How many cards are in the right pile?

11 cards  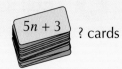 ? cards

Answer 2

a $(6n + 9) - (4n + 5) = 6n - 4n + 9 - 5 = 2n + 4$

b $(6n + 9) \div 3 = 2n + 3$

c $n + 6 = 11$ so $n = 11 - 6 = 5$
Substitute $n = 5$ into $5n + 3$ to give $25 + 3 = 28$ cards.

Exercise 11

1 Which of the following are equivalent to $12x - 18$?

    a $4(3x - 18)$ **b** $3(4x - 6)$ **c** $2(6x + 9)$

    d $6(2x - 9)$ **e** $6(2x - 3)$ **f** $-2(9 - 6x)$ *(1 mark)*

2 Which of the following are equivalent to $4xy(3x + 8y)$

    a $12xy + 32xy^2$ **b** $12x^2y + 12xy^2$ **c** $12x^2y + 32xy^2$

    d $2x(6xy + 16y^2)$ **e** $x(12y + 32)$ **f** $7x^2y + 12xy^2$ *(1 mark)*

3 a Look at this rectangle. Write an expression as simply as possible for:

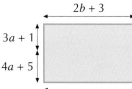 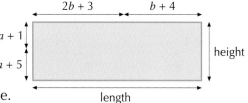

    i the height of the rectangle.   *(1 mark)*
    ii the length of the rectangle.   *(1 mark)*

b Write an expression for each missing length in the rectangle on the right.

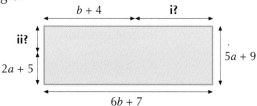

    (2 marks)

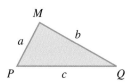

4 A triangle has sides of length a, b and c, all measured in centimetres.

$a = 5$	The side PM is 5 cm long
$a + b + c = 12$	**i**
$c = 3a$	**ii**
$a = b - 2$	**iii**

Write in words the meaning of each equation. The first one has been done for you.   *(3 marks)*

Further work on simplification can be found in Book 8.1 Page 55
Book 8.2 Page 57
Book 8.3 Page 65

12 Functions and inverse functions

KEY FACTS

○ A function is a rule that changes a number, called the input, into another number, called the output.

○ Any operation can be used in a function, such as +, −, ×, ÷, square or square root.

○ Functions can be written as mappings: for example, $x \rightarrow 3x + 1$ or as a flowchart: for example,

function

Input $\longrightarrow$ | × 3 | $\longrightarrow$ | + 1 | $\longrightarrow$ Output

○ Inverse functions reverse the direction of the function and the operations. In other words the output is brought back to the input. For example:

Input $\longleftarrow$ | ÷ 3 | $\longleftarrow$ | − 1 | $\longleftarrow$ Output

Inverse function is | x | $\longrightarrow$ | $\dfrac{x - 1}{3}$ |

Example 1 ▶   Find the inverse function of $x \rightarrow 5x - 4$.

Answer 1

function

Input $\longrightarrow$ | × 5 | $\longrightarrow$ | − 4 | $\longrightarrow$ Output

function

Input $\longleftarrow$ | ÷ 5 | $\longleftarrow$ | + 4 | $\longleftarrow$ Output

Inverse function is $x \rightarrow \dfrac{x + 4}{5}$

It is a good idea to insert numbers to check your answer. For example:

$x \rightarrow 5x - 4$ $\qquad\qquad x \rightarrow \dfrac{x + 4}{5}$

$\mathbf{7} \rightarrow (5 \times 7) - 4 = 31$ $\qquad \mathbf{31} \rightarrow (31 + 4) \div 5 = 7$

Example 2 ▶   The diagram shows one way to change pints into litres.

a   Change 21 pints into litres.   b   Change 32 litres into pints.

Answer 2   a $21 \times 4 = 84$ $84 \div 7 = 12$
So 21 pints is the same as 12 litres.

b $\longleftarrow$ ÷4 $\longleftarrow$ ×7 $\longleftarrow$

$32 \times 7 = 224$ $224 \div 4 = 56$
So 32 litres is the same as 56 pints.

Exercise 12

1 Which of the following would be the inverse function for $x \rightarrow 3x - 2$?

$x \rightarrow -3x + 2$ $\qquad$ $x \rightarrow \frac{x}{3} + 2$ $\qquad$ $x \rightarrow \frac{x + 2}{3}$ $\qquad$ $x \rightarrow -2x + 3$ $\qquad$ *(1 mark)*

2 The diagram shows one way to change °C into °F.

$$°C \rightarrow \boxed{÷5} \rightarrow \boxed{×9} \rightarrow \boxed{+32} \rightarrow °F$$

a Change 25°C into °F. *(1 mark)*

b Change 59°F into °C. *(1 mark)*

3 Tom is thinking of a number.

> I think of a number. I double it and then add 5. My answer is 19.

What is the number? *(1 mark)*

4 In a sale all items are reduced by 10%.

The diagram shows a method for working out the sale price.

a The original price of a shirt is £18.
Use the diagram to work out the sale price. *(1 mark)*

b The sale price of a dress is £27.
Which calculation will work out the original price of the dress? *(1 mark)*

$\boxed{27 \times 0.9}$ $\qquad$ $\boxed{27 ÷ 0.9}$ $\qquad$ $\boxed{27 \times 1.9}$ $\qquad$ $\boxed{27 ÷ 0.1}$

Further work on inverse functions can be found in Book 9.1 Page 41
Book 9.2 Page 8
Book 8.3 Page 91, Book 9.3 Page 8

13 Solving linear equations

LEVEL 6

KEY FACTS

○ An equation always contains an equals sign.

○ Equations work like a balancing scale. The amount on one side equals the amount on the other side.

○ Whatever operation (+, −, × or ÷) is carried out on one side of the equation must also be carried out on the other side of the equation.

○ Solving an equation involves finding the value of the unknown letter.

Example 1 ▷   Solve the equation $3m - 5 = 7$.

Answer 1   Add 5 to both sides to give: $3m - 5 + 5 = 7 + 5$

Since $-5 + 5 = 0$ and $7 + 5 = 12$, this simplifies to $3m = 12$

Divide both sides by 3 to find the answer: $m = 4$

Example 2 ▷   Jack is x years old. He says that if he multiplies his age by 3 and subtracts 2, he gets the same answer as when he adds 6 and then doubles his answer.

×3 - 2   + 6 then double

This equation shows the information: $3x - 2 = 2(x + 6)$

Solve the equation to work out Jack's age.

Answer 2   First, multiply out the bracket: $3x - 2 = 2x + 12$

Next, subtract $2x$ from both sides to give: $3x - 2 - 2x = 2x + 12 - 2x$

Simplify $3x - 2x = x$ and $2x - 2x = 0$, to give: $x - 2 = 12$

Now add 2 from both sides to give: $x - 2 + 2 = 12 + 2$

Therefore, $x = 14$

Exercise 13

1   Look at the following table.

Write in words the meaning of each equation below.

The first one has been done for you.

	Number of pencils
Red	r
Green	g
Blue	b

$r = 7$	The number of red pencils is 7.
$r + g = 11$	
$b = 3r$	
$b - g = 17$	

(3 marks)

2 Solve the following equations. Show your working.

a $2p + 5 = 9$ (1 mark)

b $6m - 7 = 11$ (1 mark)

c $3y + 5 = y + 17$ (2 marks)

d $10x + 14 = 8x + 13$ (2 marks)

3 The following diagram shows a rectangle. The area of the rectangle is 41 cm^2.

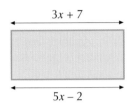

Calculate the value of x and use it to find the length and width of the rectangle. (2 marks)

4 The diagram below shows some bricks. The bricks on the bottom row add up to the same value as the brick on the top row.

	$4x$	
$x + 10$		$x - 4$

By writing down an equation, calculate the value of x. (2 marks)

5 Billy has four piles of cards containing $x - 1$, $2(x + 3)$, $x + 7$, $2y - 5$ cards.

Pile A   Pile B   Pile C   Pile D

a The total number of cards in Pile A and B is 23.
Use this information to set up an equation.
Then work out the value of x. (2 marks)

b The number of cards in Piles C and D are equal.
Use this information to work out the value of y. (1 mark)

Further work on solving equations can be found in Book 9.1 Pages 43–48, 166
Book 9.2 Pages 37– 42, 173
Book 9.3 Page 202

14 Algebraic expressions

KEY FACTS

- Only like terms can be combined, e.g. $2x + 5x = 7x$. Unlike terms such as $2x + 5y$ cannot be simplified.
- Numbers in front of letters are called coefficients.
- A single letter has a coefficient (which does not need to be written) of 1, e.g. $a = 1a$.
- $3ab$ and $5ba$ are like terms as $ab = ba$.
- When expressions have different terms, collect like terms together before simplifying. So $3a + 5b - 3 + 2a - b - 6$ is rewritten as $3a + 2a + 5b - b - 3 - 6 = 5a + 4b - 9$.

Example 1

Here are six cards with algebraic expressions on them.

$2x - 2$	$3x + 4$	$5x + 1$	$2x + 3x$	$2(x - 1)$	$3(x + 2)$
Card **A**	Card **B**	Card **C**	Card **D**	Card **E**	Card **F**

a Which two cards have **equivalent** expressions?

b What algebraic expression do you get from Card **C** – Card **A**?

c The sum of which two cards gives the expression $6x + 10$?

d Explain why there is no value of x so that Card **C** = Card **D**.

Answer 1

a $2(x - 1) = 2x - 2$ when it is expanded, so Card **A** and Card **E** are equivalent.

b $5x + 1 - (2x - 2) = 5x + 1 - 2x + 2 = 3x + 3$

c $3(x + 2) + 3x + 4 = 3x + 6 + 3x + 4 = 6x + 10$, so Cards **B** and **F**.

d If Card **C** = Card **D** then $5x + 1 = 5x$ which is impossible.

Example 2

Jack has $4x + 8$ cards divided into four packs of cards.

How many cards are in the fourth pack?

a **i**  **ii**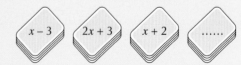

b Each of the packs below has the same number of cards.

How many cards are in each pack?

Answer 2 **a** **i** The three packs have a total of $x + x + 3 + x - 2 = 3x + 1$.
$4x + 8 - (3x + 1) = 4x - 3x + 8 - 1 = x + 7$.
The fourth pack has $x + 7$ cards.

ii The three packs have a total of $x - 3 + 2x + 3 + x + 2 = 4x + 2$.
$4x + 8 - (4x + 2) = 4x - 4x + 8 - 2 = 6$
The fourth pack has 6 cards.

b Each pack contains $(4x + 8) \div 4 = x + 2$ cards.

Exercise 14

1 The top row of this table shows some algebraic expressions.
The second row shows some mathematical operations.
Write the result of applying this operation to the expression.
The first two have been done to help you.

x	$2x$	$3x$	$x + 4$	$2x - 3$	$4x + 2$	$2(x + 3)$	$3x + 1$
Subtract 1	Multiply by 2	Add 5	Subtract 5	Subtract x	Divide by 2	Multiply by 3	Multiply by 4
$x - 1$	$4x$						

(6 marks)

2 In these walls each brick is made by adding together the two bricks below it. For example:

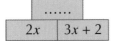

Write the missing expressions in the walls below as simply as possible.

a

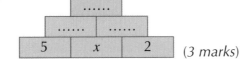

(1 mark)

b

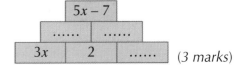

(1 mark)

c
(3 marks)

d
(3 marks)

3 **a** What is the perimeter of this rectangle?
Write your answer as simply as possible.

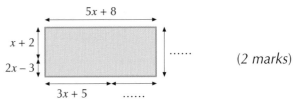

(2 marks)

b Write an expression for the missing lengths in this rectangle.

(2 marks)

4 Simplify these expressions.

a $2a + 3 + 7a - 5$ **b** $2(3a + 1)$ **c** $3(2a + 1) + 2(a - 4)$ *(3 marks)*

Further work on algebraic expressions can be found in Book 8.1 Page 55, Book 9.1 Page 149
Book 8.2 Page 57, Book 9.2 Page 156
Book 8.3 Page 65, Book 9.3 Page 183

15 Expansion of brackets

KEY FACTS

○ When two brackets are expanded or multiplied together, each term in the first bracket is multiplied with each term in the second bracket.

For example:

$$(x + 2)(x + 3) = x(x + 3) + 2(x + 3)$$
$$= x^2 + 3x + 2x + 6$$
$$= x^2 + 5x + 6$$

○ One way to remember how to expand two brackets is to use the acronym FOIL:
- multiply together the **F**irst terms in each bracket
- multiply together the **O**uter terms in the brackets
- multiply together the **I**nner terms in the brackets
- multiply together the **L**ast terms in each bracket.

Example 1 ▷ Expand the brackets for the following.

 a $(x + 6)(x − 4)$ **b** $(x − 5)(x + 2)$ **c** $(x −3)^2$

Answer 1   **a** $(x + 6)(x − 4) = x^2 − 4x + 6x − 24 = x^2 + 2x − 24$

     b $(x − 5)(x + 2) = x^2 + 2x − 5x − 10 = x^2 − 3x − 10$

     c $(x −3)^2 = (x −3)(x −3) = x^2 − 3x − 3x + 9 = x^2 − 6x + 9$

Example 2 ▷ Show that the area of the rectangle on the right is $x^2 + 9x + 20$ by splitting it into four smaller rectangles.

$x + 5$

$x + 4$

Answer 2   The rectangle can be split as follows:

The area of the rectangle is $(x + 5)(x + 4)$.

This is the same as the area of the four rectangles: $x^2 + 5x + 4x + 20 = x^2 + 9x + 20$

	x	5
x	x^2	$5x$
4	$4x$	20

Exercise 15

1 Expand the brackets for the following.

 a $(a + 6)(a + 3)$ **b** $(b + 1)(b − 4)$ **c** $(c − 6)(c + 7)$

 d $(d − 5)(d − 4)$ **e** $(e − 2)^2$ **f** $(3 − f)(5 + f)$ *(12 marks)*

2 a Which expression below is the same as $x^2 + 10x + 24$? *(1 mark)*

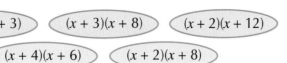

$(x + 2)(x + 3)$ $(x + 3)(x + 8)$ $(x + 2)(x + 12)$

$(x + 4)(x + 6)$ $(x + 2)(x + 8)$

b Multiply out the expression $(y - 2)(y - 9)$. *(2 marks)*

3 Show that the area of the triangle below is $\frac{1}{2}p^2 + 8p + 30$.

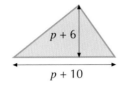

$p + 6$

$p + 10$

(2 marks)

4 The rectangle below is $(n + 6)$ cm long and $(n + 3)$ cm wide.

It has been split into four smaller rectangles.

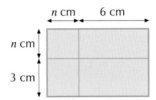

n cm   6 cm

n cm

3 cm

a Find the area of each small rectangle. *(2 marks)*

b Write down the expansion of $(n + 6)(n + 3)$. *(1 mark)*

5 Liam says:

Show that Liam is wrong.

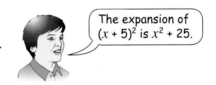

The expansion of $(x + 5)^2$ is $x^2 + 25$.

(2 marks)

6 a Show that $(x + y)(x - y) = x^2 - y^2$. *(2 marks)*

b Use this expansion to find each of the following without squaring any numbers.

  i $18^2 - 17^2$ **ii** $45^2 - 35^2$ **iii** $56^2 - 44^2$ *(3 marks)*

Further work on expansion of brackets can be found in Book 9.3 Page 188

16 Factorising

KEY FACTS

- Factors of a number divide exactly into the original number.
  For example, factors of the number 12 are 1, 2, 3, 4, 6 and 12.
- Factorising is the reverse of multiplying out brackets.
  For example, multiplying out $3(4x + 2) = 12x + 6$;
  factorising $12x + 6 = 3(4x + 2)$.
- To factorise is to take out common factors from each term.
  For example, the common factors of $3y^2 - 6y$ are 3 and y.
  Factorising $3y^2 - 6y = 3y(y - 2)$.

Example 1 ▷ The box contains six expressions.
Write down the equivalent pairs.

$2x + 6$	$x^2 + 6x$	$x(x + 6)$
	$x^2 + 3x$ $2(x + 3)$	$x(x + 3)$

Answer 1 $2x + 6 = 2(x + 3)$ $\qquad$ $x^2 + 6x = x(x + 6)$ $\qquad$ $x^2 + 3x = x(x + 3)$

Example 2 ▷ Prove that the sum of two different even numbers is always even.

Answer 2   Let the even numbers be $2n$ and $2m$.
$\qquad$ Sum $= 2n + 2m = 2(n + m)$

This is a multiple of 2, so it must be even.

Exercise 16

1 Which of the following are **not** factors of both $18a^2b$ and $12ab^2$?

$\quad 3ab \qquad\qquad 6a \qquad\qquad 2a^2b^2 \qquad\qquad 18ab \qquad\qquad 3b \qquad\qquad$ (*1 mark*)

2 a Which two of the expressions below are equivalent?

$\qquad 4(3a + 5) \qquad\qquad 3(4a + 20) \qquad\qquad 3(4a + 9)$

$\qquad\qquad 7(a + 9) \qquad\qquad\qquad 2(6a + 30) \qquad\qquad\qquad$ (*1 mark*)

b Which one of the expressions below is a correct factorisation
of $20b - 5$?

$\qquad 4(5b - 1) \qquad\qquad 2(10b - 3) \qquad\qquad 5(15b - 1)$

$\qquad\qquad 5(4b - 1) \qquad\qquad\qquad 5(4b - 4) \qquad\qquad\qquad$ (*1 mark*)

3 Which one of the expressions below is the odd one out? Explain your answer.

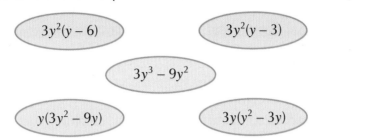

$3y^2(y - 6)$ $3y^2(y - 3)$

$3y^3 - 9y^2$

$y(3y^2 - 9y)$ $3y(y^2 - 3y)$

(1 mark)

4 **a** Factorise the following expression.
$4x + 12 = $ .... (1 mark)

b Factorise the following expression as fully as possible.
$10x^3 - 5x^2 = $ .... (1 mark)

5 The diagram below shows a parallelogram.

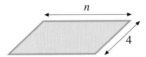

Alan says the perimeter is $2n + 8$. Beth says the perimeter is $2(n + 4)$.
Which of the following statements is correct?

Both Alan and Beth are right. Both Alan and Beth are wrong.
Alan is right and Beth is wrong. Alan is wrong and Beth is right. (1 mark)

6 Shaun thinks that the sum of three consecutive integers is always
a multiple of 3.

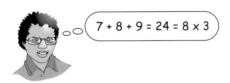

$7 + 8 + 9 = 24 = 8 \times 3$

Use algebra to show that he is right. (2 marks)

7 **a** Simplify $n + n + 1 + n + 2 + n + 3$. (1 mark)
b Factorise $4n + 6$. (1 mark)
c Prove that the sum of four consecutive numbers is even. (1 mark)

Further work on factorising can be found in Book 9.2 Page 119
Book 9.3 Page 186

17 **Substitution**

LEVEL **6, 7**

KEY FACTS

○ Substitution involves replacing variables with values in an algebraic formula.

○ When substituting into a formula, remember that the rules of BODMAS still apply.

○ Rules of algebra need careful attention. For example,
$3a = 3 \times a$, $a^2 = a \times a$, $\frac{a}{2} = a \div 2$, $3a^2 = 3 \times a^2$

Example 1 ▷

The formula for the approximate temperature conversion from degrees Fahrenheit (F) into degrees Celsius (C) is: $C = \frac{1}{2}(F - 32)$.

a Find C when F = 68°.

b Find C when F = 20°.

Answer 1

a $C = \frac{1}{2} \times (68 - 32) = \frac{1}{2} \times 36 = 18°C$

b $C = \frac{1}{2} \times (20 - 32) = \frac{1}{2} \times (-12) = -6°C$

Example 2 ▷

The formula for finding the longest side (or hypotenuse), h, of a right-angled triangle, given the two shorter sides a and b is
$$h = \sqrt{a^2 + b^2}$$

a Find h when $a = 8$ cm and $b = 6$ cm.

b Find h when $a = 3.5$ m and $b = 2.8$ m.

Answer 2

a $h = \sqrt{8^2 + 6^2} = \sqrt{64 + 36} = \sqrt{100} = 10$ cm

b $h = \sqrt{3.5^2 + 2.8^2} = \sqrt{12.25 + 7.84} = \sqrt{20.09} = 4.5$ m (1 dp)

Exercise 17

1 Use the formula $y = x^2 + 5$ to find y when:

a $x = 6$ b $x = -3$ c $x = 2.5$ *(3 marks)*

2 Use the formula $a = \dfrac{2b^2 - 4}{2}$ to find a when:

a $b = 4$ b $b = -2$ c $b = 1.6$ *(3 marks)*

3 The formula $F = \dfrac{9C + 32}{5}$ is the exact conversion to convert temperatures from degrees Celsius, C, into degrees Fahrenheit, F.

Use the formula to find the Fahrenheit temperature for each of the following.

a The freezing point of water: 0°C.

b The boiling point of water: 100°C.

c The normal body temperature: 37.1°C.

d The temperature of a freezer: –8°C. *(4 marks)*

4 The cost of a phone call is calculated by using the formula:

$$P = \frac{t + 30}{20}$$

where P is the cost in pence and t is the length of the call in seconds.

a Jane is on the phone for 5 minutes. Calculate the cost of her call. *(2 marks)*

b John makes a phone call which costs 9p. How long was he on the phone? *(2 marks)*

5 The cost to enter a theme park is given by the formula: $E = 8.5a + 4.5c$, where E is the entry cost, a is the number of adults and c is the number of children.

a Calculate the cost for six children and three adults to enter the park. *(2 marks)*

b Mr and Mrs Hardy and their children go to the park and the cost is £35. How many children do Mr and Mrs Hardy have? *(2 marks)*

6 The formula for finding the sum, S, of the first n positive numbers, $1 + 2 + 3 + 4 + \ldots\ldots + n$, is given by:

$$S = \frac{n(n + 1)}{2}$$

Use the formula to find the sum of:

a the first 10 positive numbers

b the first 50 positive numbers

c the first 1000 positive numbers. *(3 marks)*

7 The formula for finding the velocity, v, in metres per second, of an object is given by:

$v = \sqrt{u^2 + 2as}$ where u is the initial velocity, a is the acceleration and s is the distance travelled.

Calculate v for the following, giving your answer to one decimal place.

a $u = 10$, $a = 3$ and $s = 40$ *(2 marks)*

b $u = 40$, $a = -4$ and $s = 20$ *(2 marks)*

Further work on substitution can be found in Book 9.1 Page 38
Book 9.2 Page 161

18 Proof and explanation

KEY FACTS

- If you are asked to provide a proof or an explanation for a mathematical statement you need to adopt a logical approach.
- You should always give a reason for anything you write down and should never expect the marker to assume something just because it is 'obvious'.
- Try to use mathematical symbols and notation rather than words. For example, use the symbol '∴' for 'therefore' and '⇒' for 'it follows that'.
- Keep explanations short if you have to use words and use the correct mathematical vocabulary.
- Look for a 'clue' in the number of marks. For example, 1 mark usually means a single statement, 2 marks usually requires two statements and so on.

Example 1 ▷ P is a prime number and Q is an odd number.

For each part of the question, choose the statement that is true.

a PQ is always odd

PQ is always even

PQ could be odd or even

b P(Q–1) is always odd

P(Q–1) is always even

P(Q–1) could be odd or even

Answer 1 **a** Although most prime numbers are odd, there is one even prime number, 2.

∴ PQ could be odd × odd = odd or even × odd = even,

⇒ PQ could be odd or even.

b If Q is odd, then Q – 1 is even, no matter what value P has.

∴ P(Q – 1) is odd × even or even × even,

⇒ P(Q – 1) is always even.

Example 2 ▷ Prove that there is only one triangle that:

Has one right angle

Has a perimeter of 12 cm

Has three sides that are all whole numbers in centimetres

Answer 2 As the perimeter of the triangle is 12 cm and the sides have to be whole centimetres, the sides could only be either 2 cm, 5 cm, 5 cm or 3 cm, 4 cm, 5 cm or 4 cm, 4 cm, 4 cm.

If the triangle has a right angle, the sides will obey Pythagoras' theorem.

$5^2 + 2^2 \neq 5^2$, $4^2 + 4^2 \neq 4^2$, but $3^2 + 4^2 = 5^2$

Hence, the triangle with sides 3 cm, 4 cm and 5 cm obeys all three conditions.

Exercise 18

1 n is an integer.
Say whether each of the following statements is true or false.
Give an example each time to justify your choice.

    a $n(n + 1)$ is always odd   *(1 mark)*

    b $n(n+1)(n + 2)$ is always even   *(1 mark)*

    c $n^2 + 1$ can be odd or even   *(1 mark)*

2 For each part of the question, write down the statement that is true.

    a **i**   When x is odd, x^2 is odd.   **ii** When x is odd, x^2 is even.

                 Show how you know it is true for all odd values of x.   *(1 mark)*

    b **i**   When x is odd, $(x - 1)(x + 1)$ is odd.

         ii When x is odd, $(x - 1)(x + 1)$ is even.

                 Show how you know the statement is true for all odd values of x.   *(1 mark)*

3 This is part of Sandra's homework. $\dfrac{40.7 \times 56.5}{32.7 - 8.3} = 94.2$ (to 1 dp)

    By using estimation decide whether or not the answer could be right.
Show your calculations.   *(3 marks)*

4 For each of the following statements, find a value for x that makes that
statement true.

    a $x^2 < x$ **b** $x^2 = x$ **c** $x^2 > x$ *(3 marks)*

5 A quadrilateral can be split into two triangles.
A pentagon can be split into three triangles.

    a   What is the angle sum of an octagon?   *(1 mark)*

    b   Explain why the following rule is true for the angle sum of a
n-sided polygon.
Angle sum = $(n - 2) \times 180$ *(2 marks)*

6 **a**   Explain why you cannot make a triangle using the three sticks
shown below.

                9 cm   5 cm   3 cm   *(1 mark)*

    b   Think about triangles that have:

           A perimeter of 13 cm
Two equal sides
Each side a whole number of centimetres

        Prove that there are only three possible triangles that obey all
three rules.   *(2 marks)*

19 Graphs from real-life

KEY FACTS

○ Average speed can be found from a travel graph

$$\text{average speed} = \frac{\text{total distance travelled}}{\text{total time}}$$

○ When reading from a real-life graph, do check that you have the scale correct, they often step up in twos or fives.

○ A time series graph is any graph that shows data over a particular period of time.

○ Two graphs will often be drawn on the same grid in order to compare information.

Example 1 ▷

This graph shows the daytime temperature in Sheffield on one day in March.

a For how many of the hours shown was the temperature lower than 0°C?

b What is the difference between the highest and the lowest temperatures shown?

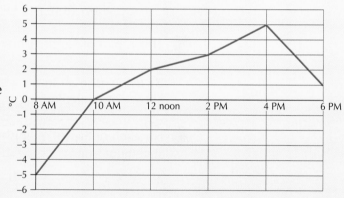

Answer 1

a The temperature was below 0°C between 8AM and 10AM which is 2 hours.

b The highest temperature is 5°C and the lowest is −5°C. The difference is therefore 5 − −5 = 10°C.

Example 2 ▷

The graph shows rainfall data for London and Manchester in 2004.

a Which place generally has the most rainfall? Explain your answer.

b In which month is there the least amount of rainfall in London?

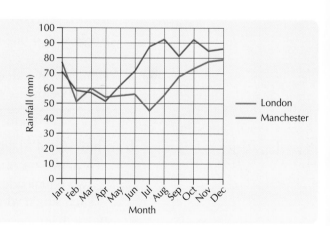

Answer 2

a As you can see from the graph, Manchester has the most rainfall because there is more rainfall there in every month except March and April.

b July

Exercise 19

1 Motorists need to know the smallest distance they should leave between moving cars.

These distances are different for bad weather and good weather conditions.

The graph shows these distances.

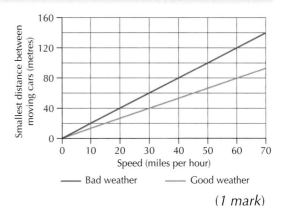

a What is the smallest distance to leave travelling at 40 mph in bad weather?

(1 mark)

b What is the smallest distance to leave travelling at 30 mph in good weather?

(1 mark)

c You are driving in good weather at 60 mph just in the safe limit, when the weather suddenly turns bad. By how much must you increase the space between the car in front?

(1 mark)

2 This graph shows the average weight of baby guinea pigs.

Using the graph, copy and complete the following table to show approximately how much an average guinea pig grows between 5 and 40 days.

(3 marks)

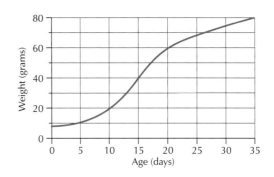

Age (days)	Approximate weight at start (g)	Approximate weight at end (g)	Approximate growth (g)
5 to 15	12	40	28
15 to 25	40	**i**?	**ii**?
25 to 35	**iii**?	**iv**?	**v**?

3 Paul and George run a 1000 metre race.

The distance–time graph shows what happened in the race.

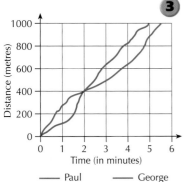

a Who led the race after 1 minute?

(1 mark)

b How far had they run when they were level with each other?

(1 mark)

c Who won the race and what was his total time?

(1 mark)

d How much later did the other person finish?

(1 mark)

Further work on real-life graphs can be found in Book 8.1 Pages 85 and 157
Book 8.2 Page 89
Book 8.3 Page 98

20 Graphs of linear equations

KEY FACTS

○ An equation is a formula that is true for all points on a graph. For example, on the graph of $y = 2x$, the y coordinate is always double the x coordinate.

○ A linear equation can be written in the form $y = mx + c$: for example, $y = 3x + 5$. It can also be written in the form $ax + by = c$: for example, $x + y = 6$.

○ m is the gradient, which is a measure of how steep the line is and c is the y intercept, i.e. the point where the graph crosses the y-axis.

Example 1 ▷ The graph on the right shows a straight line.

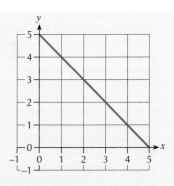

a In the table below, write the coordinates of four points on the line. Then complete the table by calculating $x + y$.

(x, y)	(,)	(,)	(,)	(,)
$x + y$				

b Write down the equation of the straight line.

c On a new grid, draw two straight lines with equations $x = 3$ and $y = 2$.

Write down the coordinates of the point where the two lines cross.

Answer 1

a

(x, y)	(0, 5)	(1, 4)	(2, 3)	(5, 0)
$x + y$	5	5	5	5

b The equation is $x + y = 5$.

c

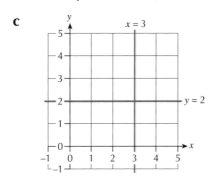

The coordinates of the point where the two lines cross is (3, 2).

Exercise 20

1 This graph shows a straight line.
The equation of the line is $y = 2x + 1$.

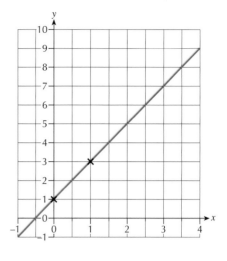

    a Does the point (20,41) lie on the
straight line?
Explain how you know. *(1 mark)*

    b Write down the coordinates of
the point where the line $y = 6$
meets the line $y = 2x + 1$. *(1 mark)*

    c Write down the equation of a
line that is parallel to the line
$y = 2x + 1$. *(1 mark)*

2 The admission price to a cinema is £5.10 per person.

    a Copy and complete the following table.

Number of people	0	10	20	30
Total cost of admission	0	£51		

    (1 mark)

    b Draw a graph to show this information. Join the points with a
straight line. *(2 marks)*

    c Use your graph to work out the total cost of admission for 25 people. *(1 mark)*

3 **a** Copy the graph below and write the equations of each line. *(4 marks)*

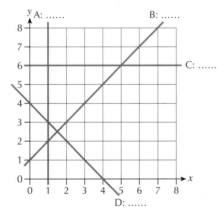

    b Which **two** lines will meet the line $y = 2x$ at the same point?
Explain your answer. *(1 mark)*

Further work on graphs of linear equations can be found in

Book 9.1 Pages 13, 123, 157
Book 8.2 Pages 85, 87, Book 9.2 Page 164
Book 8.3 Page 93

21 Solving inequalities

KEY FACTS

○ < (less than) and > (greater than) are strict inequalities because they do not include the boundary. For example, $x < 3$ means x can take any value less than 3 but not 3 itself.

○ ≤ (less than or equal to) and ≥ (greater than or equal to) mean that the boundary point is included. For example, $x ≥ 3$ means x can take any value greater than 3 and 3 itself.

○ Inequalities can be shown on number lines. A strict inequality would have an open circle as the boundary and an inclusive inequality would have a shaded circle as the boundary.

○ Graphical inequalities such as $y ≤ 2x + 3$ give a region on one side of the boundary line $y = 2x + 3$.

○ A strict graphical inequality such as $2x + 3y > 6$ would have a dotted boundary line to show that it is not included.

Example 1 ▷

Four points are
$A(3, 1)$, $B(4, 1)$, $C(2, 5)$, $D(2, 1)$.

Write down the point or points that obey the inequalities given.

The first line is done for you.

	Inequality	Points
	$x > 2$ is true for points	A, B
a	$y < 3$ is true for points	
b	$x + y ≥ 4$ is true for points	
c	$y + 2x > 6$ is true for points	

Answer 1

a   The y coordinate is the second value. It is less than 3 for points A, B and D.

b $x + y$ is the sum of both coordinates. $x + y ≥ 4$ for points A, B and C.

c $y + 2x$ is double the first coordinate plus the second.
   $y + 2x > 6$ for points A, B and C.

Example 2 ▷

A teacher wants her class to find a point on the grid by asking questions about inequalities.

Use the questions and the answers in the table to identify the point.

Question	Answer
Is $x > 0$?	No
Is $x + y > 1$?	Yes
Is $y < 3$?	Yes

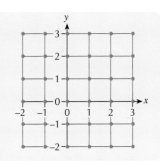

Answer 2

If x is not greater than 0, then all points to the right of the y axis are eliminated.
If $x + y$ is greater than 1 then the only points that are true are $(0, 2)$, $(0, 3)$, $(-1, 3)$.
If $y < 3$ the only point from the three above is $(0, 2)$.
Hence the point is $(0, 2)$.

Exercise 21

1 The number line below shows the set of numbers $-2 < x \leq 3$.

a Write down the set of numbers shown on this number line.

(1 mark)

b Write down the set of numbers shown on this number line.

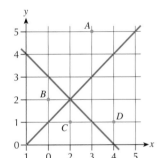

(1 mark)

c Write down an integer that is in both sets of numbers in parts **a** and **b**. *(1 mark)*

2 a Solve the equation $2x + 7 = 13$. *(1 mark)*

b Which of the following is the solution to the inequality $2x + 7 > 13$?

$x \geq 3$ $\qquad$ $x < 3$ $\qquad$ $x > 3$ $\qquad$ $x \leq 3$ *(1 mark)*

c Which of the following is the solution to the inequality $7 - 2x > 13$?

$x > -3$ $\qquad$ $x < 3$ $\qquad$ $x > 3$ $\qquad$ $x < -3$ *(1 mark)*

3 The graph shows the lines $y = x$ and $x + y = 4$.

Copy and complete the table below with the points that obey the inequalities at the top of each row and at the side of each column.

One has been done for you.

	$x + y > 4$	$x + y < 4$
$y > x$	A	
$y < x$		

(3 marks)

4 If $n^2 < 25$ then n is between -5 and $+5$. So $-5 < n < 5$.

Write down the solution set to the following inequalities.

a $n^2 \leq 36$ $\qquad$ **b** $n^2 < 100$ *(2 marks)*

5 If $n^2 \geq 4$, then n is bigger than or equal to 2 or smaller than or equal to -2.
So $n \geq 2$ or $n \leq -2$.

Write down the solution set to the following inequalities.

a $n^2 \geq 9$ $\qquad$ **b** $n^2 > 25$ *(2 marks)*

6 Solve the inequalities **a** $x - 5 > 13$ **b** $5x + 1 \leq 11$ **c** $3 - 2x < 5$. *(3 marks)*

Further work on solving inequalities can be found in Book 9.3 Page 50

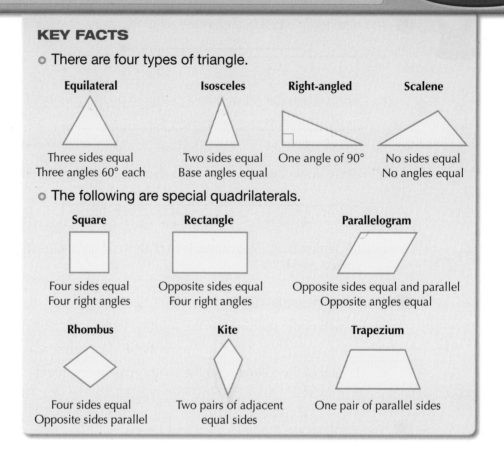

KEY FACTS

○ There are four types of triangle.

Equilateral

Three sides equal
Three angles 60° each

Isosceles

Two sides equal
Base angles equal

Right-angled

One angle of 90°

Scalene

No sides equal
No angles equal

○ The following are special quadrilaterals.

Square

Four sides equal
Four right angles

Rectangle

Opposite sides equal
Four right angles

Parallelogram

Opposite sides equal and parallel
Opposite angles equal

Rhombus

Four sides equal
Opposite sides parallel

Kite

Two pairs of adjacent
equal sides

Trapezium

One pair of parallel sides

Example 1 ▷

> I am thinking of a quadrilateral that has two pairs of parallel sides but no right angles.

a What type of quadrilateral is Jonathan thinking of?

b Name a **different** quadrilateral that Jonathan could be thinking of?

Answer 1

a and **b** There are two quadrilaterals that Jonathan could be thinking of: a parallelogram or a rhombus.

Exercise 22

1 a On a centimetre-square grid draw a quadrilateral which has exactly one pair of parallel sides. *(1 mark)*

b Now draw an isosceles right-angled triangle. *(1 mark)*

2 Look at the three diagrams below.

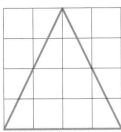 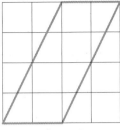 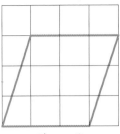

Shape **A**   Shape **B**   Shape **C**

    a   Is Shape **A** an isosceles triangle? Explain your answer.   *(1 mark)*

    b   Is Shape **B** a parallelogram? Explain your answer.   *(1 mark)*

    c   Is Shape **C** a rhombus? Explain your answer.   *(1 mark)*

3 **a**   The diagram below shows part of a kite. Copy and complete the kite.   *(1 mark)*

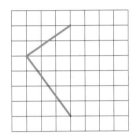

    b   The diagram below shows part of a parallelogram. Copy and complete the parallelogram.   *(1 mark)*

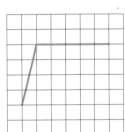

4 Copy and complete the following sentences.

    a   In an equilateral triangle every angle is ......° and all the sides are ....   *(1 mark)*

    b   In a rectangle every angle is ......° and .... sides are ....   *(1 mark)*

Further work on triangles and quadrilaterals can be found in Book 7.1 Pages 122
Book 7.2 Page 120
Book 7.3 Page 132

23 Angles in a polygon

KEY FACTS

- Polygons are straight-sided shapes such as triangles and quadrilaterals.
- In a regular polygon all sides and angles are the same.
- The sum of the angles in any polygon is always constant. For example, all triangles have an angle sum of 180°, all pentagons have an angle sum of 540°.
- The rule for the angle sum in an n-sided polygon is $(n - 2) \times 180$.
- The exterior angles of all polygons have a sum of 360°.
- The interior angle of a regular n-sided polygon is given by
$$\frac{(n - 2) \times 180}{n}.$$
- The exterior angle of a regular n-sided polygon is given by $\frac{360}{n}$.
- The angles on a straight line add up to 180°.
- The angles at a point add up to 360°.

Example 1 ▷ The diagram shows the side view of a cuboid resting on an isosceles triangle.

Work out the values of the angles a, b and c.

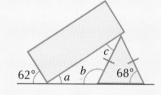

Answer 1 Angle a can be worked out by using angles along a straight line.
$62 + 90 + a = 180$
$a = 180 - 90 - 62 = 28°$

Angle b is the external angle of the isosceles triangle.
$b = 180 - 68 = 112°$

Angle c can be worked out using angles in a triangle.
$c = 180 - 28 - 112 = 40°$

Example 2 ▷ ABCD is a parallelogram.

Calculate the angles p and q.

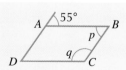

Answer 2 Angle p is an alternate angle to the angle of 55°.
Alternate angles are equal so $p = 55°$.

Angle q is an interior angle between parallel lines with angle p.
Interior angles add up to 180° so $q = 180 - 55 = 125°$.

Exercise 23

1 Work out the values of angles *a*, *b* and *c* in the following diagram.

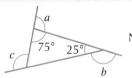

Not to scale

(3 marks)

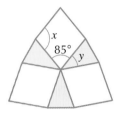

2 The shape on the left has three identical isosceles triangles and three identical rhombi.

Work out the values of the angles *x* and *y*. *(2 marks)*

3 The diagram shows an equilateral triangle.

Work out the values of angles *a* and *b*.

(2 marks)

4 A quadrilateral can be split into two triangles.

a What is the total of the angles inside a quadrilateral?

(1 mark)

b What is the total of the angles inside a hexagon?

(1 mark)

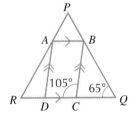

5 The diagram shows a parallelogram *ABCD* inside an isosceles triangle *PQR*.

a Angle *BQC* is 65°. Write down another angle that is 65°. *(1 mark)*

b Angle *BCD* is 105°. Write down another angle that is 105°. *(1 mark)*

c Calculate angle *CBQ*. *(1 mark)*

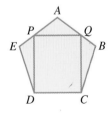

6 The diagram shows a rectangle *PQCD* inside a regular pentagon *ABCDE*.

a Write down the value of angle *DEP*. *(1 mark)*

b Work out the value of angle *QCB*. *(1 mark)*

c Work out the value of angle *APQ*. *(1 mark)*

Further work on angles in a polygon can be found in Book 9.1 Pages 55–63
Book 9.2 Pages 52, 56
Book 9.3 Page 73

24 Pythagoras' theorem

KEY FACTS

○ Pythagoras' theorem states that:

'In a right-angled triangle, the square on the hypotenuse is equal to the sum of the squares on the two smaller sides.'

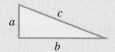

$$c^2 = a^2 + b^2$$

So, where $a = 6$ cm, $b = 8$ cm and $c = 10$ cm, Pythagoras' theorem can be used to prove that this is a right-angled triangle:
$10^2 = 100$ and $6^2 + 8^2 = 36 + 64 = 100$. Hence $c^2 = a^2 + b^2$.

○ Two common right-angled triangles to remember are 3, 4, 5 and 5, 12, 13.

Example 1 ▷

A square of side length 6 cm has been drawn inside a circle.

Calculate the diameter of the circle, giving your answer to 1 decimal place.

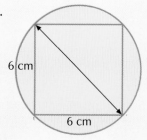

Answer 1

As the diameter forms part of a right-angled triangle it is possible to use Pythagoras' theorem to calculate its length.

The diameter of the circle will be the hypotenuse of the right-angled triangle. Therefore:

$\text{Diameter}^2 = 6^2 + 6^2 = 36 + 36 = 72$
$\text{Diameter} = \sqrt{72} = 8.4852814$ cm

The diameter of the circle is therefore 8.5 cm.

Example 2 ▷

A plane flies from Bromby to Leminly.

Leminly is 20 km to the East and 8 km to the North of Bromby.

Calculate the shortest distance from Bromby to Leminly.

Give your answer to three significant figures.

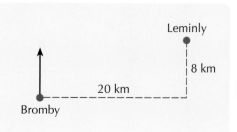

Answer 2

The shortest distance will form a right-angled triangle with the two given distances and it will be the hypotenuse. Therefore:

$\text{Distance}^2 = 20^2 + 8^2 = 400 + 64 = 464$
$\text{Distance} = \sqrt{464} = 21.540659$

The shortest distance from Bromby to Leminly is 21.5 km.

Exercise 24

1 Hope is 8.5 km to the East and 4.8 km to the North of Bridgend.

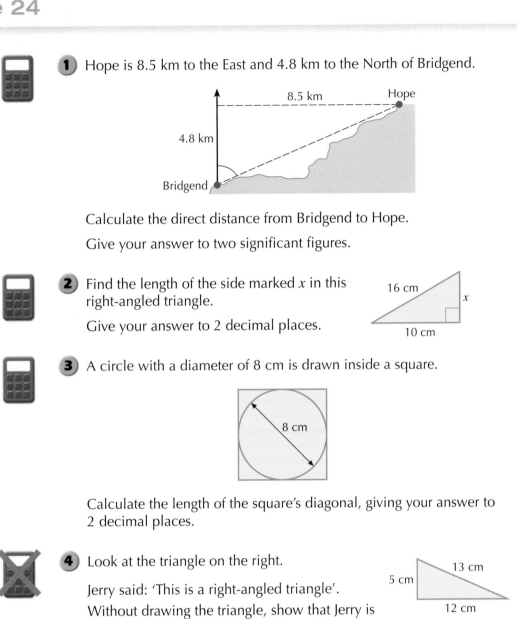

Calculate the direct distance from Bridgend to Hope.

Give your answer to two significant figures.   *(3 marks)*

2 Find the length of the side marked x in this right-angled triangle.

Give your answer to 2 decimal places.   *(2 marks)*

16 cm

x

10 cm

3 A circle with a diameter of 8 cm is drawn inside a square.

8 cm

Calculate the length of the square's diagonal, giving your answer to 2 decimal places.   *(3 marks)*

4 Look at the triangle on the right.

Jerry said: 'This is a right-angled triangle'.
Without drawing the triangle, show that Jerry is correct.   *(2 marks)*

13 cm

5 cm

12 cm

5 This is Padmini's sketch of all the paths in a park.

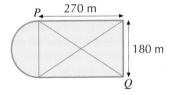

P   270 m

180 m

Q

Approximately how long is the diagonal path *PQ*?   *(2 marks)*

Further work on Pythagoras can be found in Book 9.3 Page 58

25 Circumference and area of a circle

KEY FACTS

- The radius is a straight line from the centre of a circle to its circumference. It is equivalent to half of the diameter.
- The perimeter is a line drawn around the edge of a shape. The circumference is a special name for the perimeter of a circle.
- Your calculator should have a π button. Always use it. If your calculator does not have a π button use the value 3.142.
- One formula for the circumference of a circle is $C = \pi d$, where d is the diameter. Another formula is $C = 2\pi r$, where r is the radius.
- The formula for the area of a circle is $A = \pi r^2$, where r is the radius. Work out r^2 first before multiplying by π. For example, $\pi 5^2 = \pi \times 5^2 = \pi \times 25 = 78.5$.
- Always ensure that your final answer states the correct units.

Example 1 ▶

a A circle has a radius of 25 cm.

Calculate the area of the circle to 1 decimal place.

b Another circle has a circumference of 150 cm.

Calculate the radius of the circle to 1 decimal place.

25 cm

Answer 1

a Area $= \pi r^2 = \pi \times 25^2 = \pi \times 625 = 1963.5$ cm^2

b If $C = 150$, $2\pi r = 150$
$r = 150 \div 2\pi = 23.9$ cm

Example 2 ▶

A tractor has a front wheel with a diameter of 80 cm and a rear wheel with a diameter of 170 cm.

a What is the circumference of the front wheel?

b The tractor travels 1 kilometre. How many times will the front wheel go round? Give your answer to the nearest 10.

c When the front wheel has turned 100 times, how many times will the rear wheel have turned?

Answer 2

a $C = \pi \times d = \pi \times 80 = 251.3$ cm (1 dp)

b 1 kilometre $= 100\,000$ cm
$100\,000 \div 251.3 = 397.93 = 400$ to the nearest 10

c In 100 turns the front wheel turns $100 \times \pi \times 80 = 25\,132.7$ cm.
The rear wheel has a circumference of $\pi \times 170 = 534.1$ cm.
$25\,132.7 \div 534.1 = 47$ times

Exercise 25

1 Calculate the perimeter of a semi-circle with a radius of 6 cm. *(2 marks)*

2 A bike has a front wheel with a diameter of 36 cm.

    a What is the circumference of the wheel? *(1 mark)*

    b John rides 10 kilometres. How many times does the wheel turn? Give your answer to the nearest 10. *(2 marks)*

3 Mary has a large circular dining table that has a diameter of 2.5 metres.

For a dinner party each place setting needs a minimum of 75 cm.

Mary wants to invite ten people to dinner. Will she have enough room at the table? Show your working. *(3 marks)*

4 Calculate the area of a semi-circle with a diameter of 20 cm. *(2 marks)*

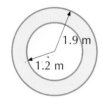

5 Calculate the shaded area shown.

The inner circle has a radius of 1.2 metres.

The outer circle has a radius of 1.9 metres. *(3 marks)*

6 **a** A circle has a diameter of 26 cm.
    Calculate the circumference of the circle. *(1 mark)*

    b Another circle has an area of 150 cm².
    Calculate the radius of the circle. *(2 marks)*

7 The diagram shows a circle and a square.

They have the same area.

The square has a side of 5 cm.

What is the diameter of the circle? *(3 marks)*

5 cm

8 The diagram shows a circle and a square.

They have the same perimeter.

The side of the square is 7 cm.

What is the radius of the circle? *(2 marks)*

7 cm

9 The diagram shows a square inside a circle of radius 10 cm.

What percentage of the circle is covered by the square? *(3 marks)*

20 cm

Further work on circumference and area of a circle can be found in Book 9.2 Pages 91, 93
Book 8.3 Pages 77, 79

26 Area of plane shapes

LEVEL 6

KEY FACTS

○ The common metric units for area are mm², cm² and m².
  It is useful to learn the following:
    $100 \text{ mm}^2 = 1 \text{ cm}^2$ $10\,000 \text{ cm}^2 = 1 \text{ m}^2$

○ The formula for the area of a rectangle is:
    $A = lw$

○ The formula for the area of a triangle is:
    $A = \dfrac{bh}{2}$

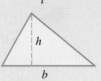

○ The formula for the area of a parallelogram is:
    $A = bh$

Example 1 ▷   A playground is 20 m long and 30 m wide. What is the area?

Answer 1   Area $= lw = 20\text{m} \times 30\text{m} = 600 \text{ m}^2$

Exercise 26

1 On a centimetre-square grid, draw rectangles with the following areas:
    a 6 cm²   **b** 10 cm²   **c** 8 cm²   **d** 20 cm²   *(4 marks)*

2 The shapes in this question are drawn on centimetre-square grids.

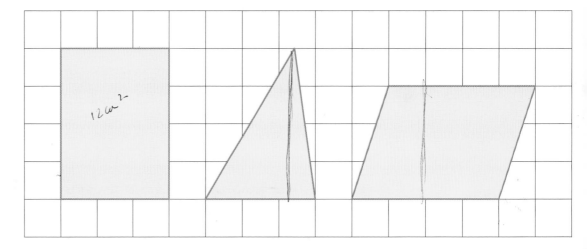

Which of the following statements is true?

A: The rectangle and the parallelogram have the same area.

B: The triangle and the parallelogram have the same area.

C: The rectangle and the triangle have the same area.

D: All the shapes have different areas.   (*1 mark*)

3 On a copy of the grid below draw a triangle that has the same area as the parallelogram.   (*1 mark*)

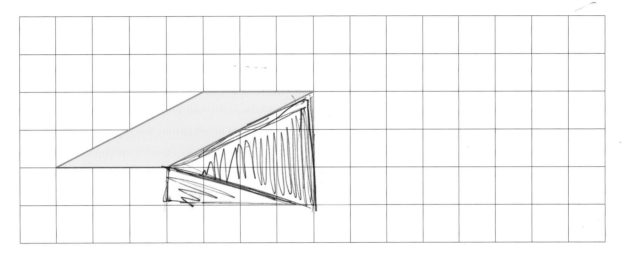

4 Which of the following shapes have an area of 8 cm²?

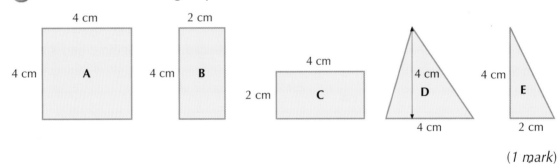

4 cm   2 cm

4 cm **A**   4 cm **B**

4 cm

2 cm **C**

4 cm **D**

4 cm

4 cm **E**

4 cm   2 cm

(*1 mark*)

Further work on areas of plane shapes can be found in

Book 8.1 Pages 63, 65, Book 9.1 Pages 87–92, 183
Book 8.2 Pages 67–73, Book 9.2 Pages 190, 192
Book 9.3 Page 220

(27) Volume of 3-D shapes   LEVEL **6, 7**

KEY FACTS

○ The common metric units for volume are mm³, cm³ and m³.
It is useful to learn the following conversions:

1000 mm³	= 1 cm³	1000 cm³ = 1 litre
1 000 000 cm³ = 1 m³		1 m³ = 1000 litres

○ The formula for the volume of a cuboid is:
$V = lwh$

○ A prism is a 3-D shape that has a uniform cross-section.
The formula for the volume of a prism is:
$V = Al$
where A is the area of the cross-section.

○ The formula for the volume of a cylinder is:
$V = \pi r^2 l$
where r is the radius of the circle.

Example 1 ▷   A fish tank has the measurements shown.

a   Calculate the volume of the tank.

b   How many litres of water can the tank hold when it is full?

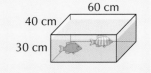

Answer 1   **a** $V = lwh = 60 \times 40 \times 30 = 72\,000$ cm³

b   1000 cm³ = 1 litre, so 72 000 ÷ 1000 = 72 litres

Example 2 ▷   A chocolate box is the shape of a triangular prism.
Calculate the volume of the box.

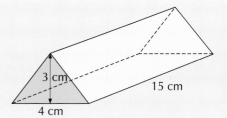

Answer 2 $V = Al$: the area of the triangular cross-section = $\frac{1}{2} \times 4 \times 3 = 6$ cm² ,
so the volume of the box = $6 \times 15 = 90$ cm³.

Exercise 27

1   Ben has a box of 24 plastic cubes. Each side of a cube measures 1 cm.
He can make only six different cuboids with the cubes.

Copy and complete the table to show the dimensions of these cuboids.

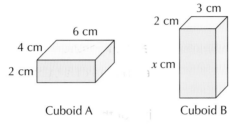

	Dimensions		
Cuboid 1	1	1	24
Cuboid 2	1	2	12
Cuboid 3			
Cuboid 4			
Cuboid 5			
Cuboid 6			

(4 marks)

2 The two cuboids below have the same volume.

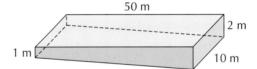

Cuboid A   Cuboid B

a Work out the volume of Cuboid A. *(2 marks)*

b What is the length marked *x* on Cuboid B? *(1 mark)*

3 The diagram on the right shows the dimensions of a swimming pool.

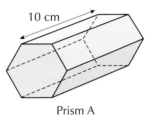

a Calculate the volume of the pool. *(2 marks)*

b How many litres of water are there in the pool when it is full? *(1 mark)*

4 The prisms A and B below have the same cross-sectional area.

10 cm   8 cm

Prism A   Prism B

Find the volume of Prism B, if the volume of Prism A is 400 cm³. *(2 marks)*

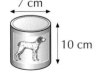

7 cm

10 cm

5 The internal measurements of a cylindrical tin of dog food are shown on the left.

Calculate the volume of the tin, giving your answer to the nearest cubic centimetre. *(2 marks)*

Further work on volume of 3-D shapes can be found in Book 9.1 Page 93
Book 9.2 Page 97
Book 9.3 Page 112

28 **Units of measurement**

KEY FACTS

○ It is useful to learn the following metric units:

| 10 mm = 1 cm | 100 cm = 1 m | 1000 m = 1 km |
| 1000 g = 1 kg | 1000 kg = 1 tonne | 1000 ml = 1 litre |

○ It is also useful to learn the following Imperial–Metric approximations:

| 1 inch | ≈ 2.5 cm | 2.2 pounds ≈ 1 kg |
| 4.5 litres ≈ 1 gallon | 5 miles | ≈ 8 km |

Example 1 ▷ How many kilometres are equivalent to 10 miles?

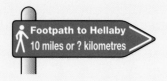

Answer 1 As 5 miles are equivalent to 8 km, 10 miles are equivalent to 16 km.

Example 2 ▷ A scale measures grams and ounces.

Use the scale to answer the following questions.

a Approximately how many grams are equal to 16 ounces?

b About how many ounces is 1 kilogram?

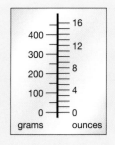

Answer 2 **a** 450 grams

b 200 grams = 7 ounces
1 kg = 5 × 200 g = 5 × 7 ounces = 35 ounces

Example 3 ▷ **a** The width of a door is 88 cm.
What is the width of the door in millimetres?

b Steve's height is 1.8 m.
What is his height in centimetres?

c The distance from Hellaby to Maltby is 2.7 km.
What is the distance from Hellaby to Maltby in metres?

Answer 3 **a** 88 × 10 = 880 mm

b 1.8 × 100 = 180 cm

c 2.7 × 1000 = 2700 m

Exercise 28

1 The same measurement is often given in different units.
For each container below state the correct missing units.
Choose your units from: grams, litres, pints, pounds, kilograms, inches.

a weight of jam

b bottle of juice

Quality
FRUIT JAM
1 **i** ...?...
450 **ii** ...?...

1.5 **i** ...?...
2.7 **ii** ...?...

(4 marks)

2 The following sign is displayed in a lift.

This lift can carry up to 1000 pounds

Seven people want to use the lift.

The seven people's weights are: 46 kg, 61 kg, 107 kg, 58 kg, 69 kg, 70 kg and 91 kg.
Sue says: 'We are too heavy to all get in the lift together.'
Is she right? Explain your answer. *(3 marks)*

3 a Baby Noah was born weighing 4 kilograms.
What was his birth weight in grams? *(1 mark)*

b Helen bought a 1.2 litre bottle of orange juice.
How much orange juice was in the bottle in millilitres? *(1 mark)*

c Nellie the small elephant weighed 1.08 tonne.
How much did she weigh in kilograms? *(1 mark)*

4 Some people use feet to measure length.

The diagram below shows one way to change feet to metres.

Number of feet ⟩ × 12 ⟩ × 2.54 ⟩ ÷ 100 ⟩ Number of metres

a Change 30 feet to metres. *(1 mark)*

b Change 60 metres to feet. *(2 marks)*

5 Steve is driving through France when he sees a speed limit sign.

What speed in miles per hour should he
not exceed to stay within the speed limit?

**Limite de Vitesse
40 km par heure**

(2 marks)

Further work on units can be found in Book 8.1 Page 72
Book 8.2 Page 77
Book 8.3 Page 84

61

Compound measures

KEY FACTS

○ Speed is a measure of how fast an object is moving. To calculate speed, two measurements are needed: distance and time. Usually, an 'average speed' is calculated over the total distance travelled.

○ Common units of speed are: metres per second (m/s), kilometres per hour (km/h) and miles per hour (mph).

A formula triangle can be used to show the connection between distance (D), speed (S) and time (T).

Covering up the quantity required leads to the formulae:

$$D = ST \qquad S = \frac{D}{T} \qquad T = \frac{D}{S}$$

○ Density is a measure of how compact an object is. To calculate density, two measurements are needed: mass and volume.

○ Common units of density are: grams per centimetre cubed (g/cm^3) and kilograms per metre cubed (kg/m^3).

A formula triangle can be used to show the connection between mass (M), density (D) and volume (V).

Covering up the quantity required leads to the formulae:

$$M = DV \qquad D = \frac{M}{V} \qquad V = \frac{M}{D}$$

○ Examples of other compound measures are: fuel consumption in kilometres per litre (km/l) and rate of flow in litres per second (l/s).

Example 1 ▷ A train leaves London at 09:30 and arrives in Manchester at 11:54. Find the average speed of the train if the total distance travelled was 180 miles.

Answer 1 $T = 2$ hours and 24 minutes. Change the minutes to a decimal by dividing the number of minutes by 60: $24 \div 60 = 0.4$, so $T = 2.4$ hours.

$$S = \frac{D}{T} = \frac{180}{2.4} = 75 \text{ mph}$$

Example 2 ▷ A block of wood has a density of 0.8 g/cm^3.

    a Find the volume of the block.

    b What is the mass of the block?

Answer 2   **a** $V = 15 \times 6 \times 4 = 360 \text{ cm}^3$

    b $M = DV = 0.8 \times 360 = 288 \text{ g}$

Exercise 29

1 Beth is taking part in a swimming competition and her time for the 200 m freestyle is 2 minutes and 5 seconds. Calculate her average speed in m/s.

(*2 marks*)

2 Matthew and Tom travel by road from Town A to Town B along different routes.

Their journey times are the same.

Matthew travels at an average speed of 50 km/h.

Calculate Tom's average speed for the journey.

(*2 marks*)

3 On average, John's car uses petrol at the rate of 1 litre for every 15 kilometres travelled.

John drives to a conference at an average speed of 60 km/h and the journey takes him $1\frac{1}{2}$ hours.

Calculate how many litres of petrol he used.

(*2 marks*)

4 Sally goes on a five-kilometre walk. The time–distance graph shows her journey.

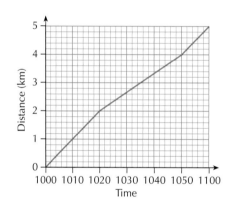

a Between 1000 and 1020, what was her speed in kilometres per hour? (*1 mark*)

b For how many minutes did she travel at this speed on the walk? (*1 mark*)

c At what speed did she start to walk at 1020? (*1 mark*)

5 A train travels between three stations X, Y and Z.

The diagram shows the distances between the stations and the times taken to complete each journey.

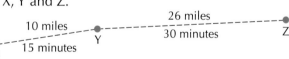

a What is the average speed of the train between X and Y? (*1 mark*)

b What is the average speed of the train between Y and Z? (*1 mark*)

c What is the average speed of the train between X and Z? (*1 mark*)

6 A water tank has a capacity of 5000 litres.

It is filled through a hosepipe, which has a rate of flow of 25 litres per minute.

How long does it take to fill the tank? Give your answer in hours and minutes. (*2 marks*)

Further work on compound measures can be found in Book 9.3 Page 114

KEY FACTS

- A transformation changes the position or size of a shape.
  The original shape is called the **object** and the transformed
  shape is the **image**.
- If the object and image are the same size and shape, the two
  shapes are said to be **congruent**.
- There are four basic types of transformation:
  - A **translation** moves a shape from one position to another.
    The object and the image are congruent.
  - A **reflection** reflects a shape in a mirror line. The object and
    the image are congruent. A mirror or tracing paper may be
    used when doing reflection questions.
  - A **rotation** turns a shape through an angle, clockwise or
    anticlockwise, about a centre of rotation. The object and the
    image are congruent. Tracing paper may be used when doing
    rotation questions.
  - An **enlargement** makes a shape bigger or smaller about a
    centre of enlargement by a scale factor. If the scale factor is
    greater than 1, the image is bigger than the object. If the scale
    factor is less than 1, the image is smaller than the object. The
    object and the image are not congruent and the shapes are
    said to be **similar**.

Example 1 ▷

Triangle *A* is shown on the coordinate grid.

a Translate triangle *A* five squares to the left and four
squares down. Label this triangle *B*.

b Reflect triangle *A* in the *y*-axis. Label this triangle *C*.

c Rotate triangle *A* 90° clockwise about the origin.
Label this triangle *D*.

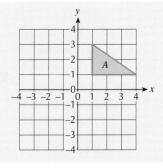

Answer 1

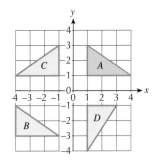

Example 2 ▷ The rectangle ABCD is shown on the coordinate grid.

Enlarge the rectangle by a scale factor 2 about the origin.
Label this rectangle A'B'C'D'.

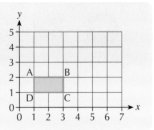

Answer 2

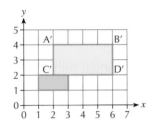

Notice that, since the enlargement is about the origin, the coordinates of the vertices of the object are multiplied by two to give the coordinates of the vertices of the image.

Exercise 30

1 Triangle P is rotated anticlockwise onto triangle Q.

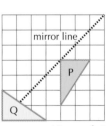

a On a copy of the diagram, put a cross to mark the centre of rotation.

b What is the angle of rotation?

c Reflect triangle P in the mirror line.

(3 marks)

2 On a copy of the coordinate grid, enlarge the triangle by a scale factor 2 about the origin.

(3 marks)

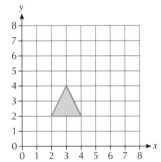

3 Pentagon B is an enlargement of pentagon A with a scale factor $\frac{1}{2}$.

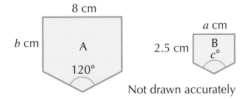

Not drawn accurately

Write down the values of *a*, *b* and *c*.

(3 marks)

4 Triangles A, B, C and D are all transformations of the shaded triangle.

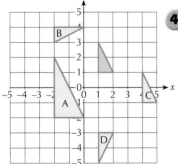

Complete each of the following statements to make them true:

a Triangle A is an …… with a scale factor …… and a centre of (…, …) *(2 marks)*

b Triangle B is a …… in a …… direction of …… degrees about a centre of (…, …) *(2 marks)*

c Triangle C is a translation of …… units right and …… units …… *(2 marks)*

d Triangle D is a …… in the line …… *(2 marks)*

Further work on transformations can be found in Book 8.1 Page 104, Book 9.1 Page 138
Book 8.2 Pages 107, 111, Book 9.2 Page 140
Book 8.3 Pages 118, 122, Book 9.3 Page 166

31 Parallel lines

LEVEL **6**

KEY FACTS

○ Two lines are parallel if they remain the same distance apart.

○ A straight line cutting a pair of parallel lines is called a **transversal**.

c and e are **alternate** angles (Z angles): they are equal to each other.

d and f are also **alternate** angles: they equal each other.

d and e are **allied** angles: they add up to 180°.

c and f are also **allied** angles: they add up to 180°.

a and e are **similar** angles, they equal each other.

b and f are also **similar** angles: they equal each other.

Example 1 ▷

The shape on the right is a parallelogram.

Work out the size of angle A.

Give a reason for your answer.

Answer 1

The two marked angles are allied so add up to 180°. Hence $A = 180 - 55 = 125°$.

Example 2 ▷

Mick has drawn a rhombus.

a Calculate the size of angle d.

b Calculate the size of angle e.

Answer 2

a The angle marked 65° and angle d are alternate angles so they are equal. Therefore, d is 65°.

b The angle marked 65° and angle e are allied angles so they add up to 180°. Therefore, e is $180 - 65 = 115°$.

Example 3 ▷

The shape below has two identical white tiles and a triangular tile in between.

a Calculate the size of angle P.

b Calculate the size of angle Q. Show your working.

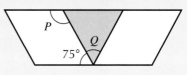

Answer 3

a P and the 75° angle are allied angles: $180 - 75 = 105°$ so $P = 105°$.

b $Q = 180 - (2 \times 75) = 30°$

Exercise 31

1 The diagram below shows a triangle drawn between two parallel lines.

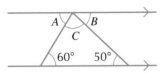

    a   Calculate the size of angle A.   (*1 mark*)

    b   Calculate the size of angle B.   (*1 mark*)

    c   Calculate the size of angle C.   (*1 mark*)

2 Billy drew a parallelogram where the large angle was **three** times the size of the small angle.

    a   What is the size of the large angle in terms of x?   (*1 mark*)

    b   Write down an equation for the sum of the two angles marked on the diagram.   (*1 mark*)

    c   Solve this equation to find the size of the small angle.   (*1 mark*)

3 Tim drew the diagram below.

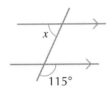

Calculate the size of angle x. Explain your answer.   (*2 marks*)

4 Sketch pairs of parallel lines and a transversal showing:

    a   a pair of identical allied angles   (*1 mark*)

    b   alternate angles of 45°.   (*1 mark*)

5 Look at the following diagram.

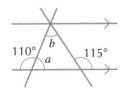

    a   Calculate the size of angle a.   (*1 mark*)

    b   Calculate the size of angle b.   (*2 marks*)

Further work on parallel lines can be found in Book 8.2 Page 19
Book 8.3 Page 19

Isometric drawings

LEVEL 5

KEY FACTS

- 3-D shapes can be drawn more accurately on an isometric grid.
- When using an isometric grid, the dots should form vertical columns.
- Hidden sides do not have to be shown on an isometric drawing.

Example 1 ▷ Draw this cuboid accurately on an isometric grid.

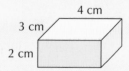

Answer 1

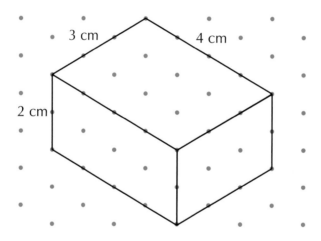

Exercise 32

You will need isometric dotty paper for this exercise.

1 Draw this cube accurately on an isometric grid.

(2 marks)

2 The cuboid below has been made using three cubes.

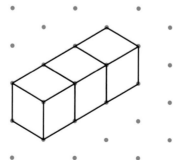

On an isometric grid, draw a cuboid that is twice as long, twice as wide and twice as high as the cuboid above.

(2 marks)

3 Four cubes have been joined together to make a shape.

The diagram shows the shape after a quarter of a turn.

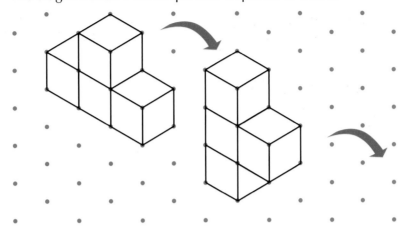

On an isometric grid, draw the shape after another quarter of a turn.   (2 marks)

4 Jackie made a letter T with six cubes and then drew the shape on an isometric grid.

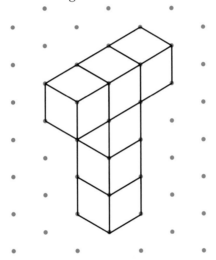

She then turned the letter upside down.

On an isometric grid, draw what the letter T looks like now.   (2 marks)

5 This 3-D shape is made from five centimetre cubes.

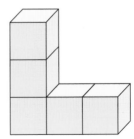

Draw the shape on an isometric grid.   (2 marks)

Further work on isometric drawings can be found in Book 8.1 Page 173
Book 8.2 Page 180
Book 8.3 Page 194

33 Solids and nets

KEY FACTS

○ A net is a flat shape that can be folded up to make a solid.

○ Solids can have several different nets. For example, the nets below can be folded up to make a cube.

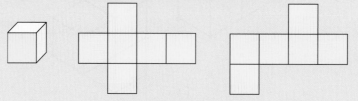

○ Sometimes nets are drawn with tabs on to show how the net can be joined together to make a solid.

Example 1 ▷

The following sketch shows the net of a pentagonal prism.

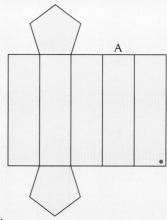

The net is folded up to make the prism.

a Which edge will meet with edge A? Label it B.

b The corner marked meets two other corners. Label the two corners.

Answer 1

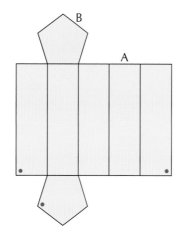

Exercise 33

1 The diagram shows an open box.

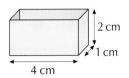

On squared paper, draw the net of the box. *(2 marks)*

2 a A trapezium is cut out of paper to make a net.

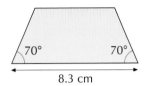

Which one of the 3-D shapes below could be made with this net? *(1 mark)*

b Make an accurate drawing of the net. *(3 marks)*

3 The sketch below shows the net of a cuboid.

The net is folded up to make a prism.

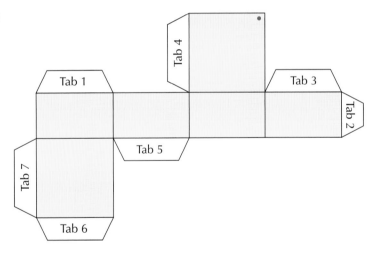

a Which edge is Tab 1 glued to?
On a copy of the diagram, label this edge A. *(1 mark)*

b Which edge is Tab 6 glued to?
Label this edge B. *(1 mark)*

c The corner marked meets two other corners.
Label these two other corners. *(1 mark)*

> Further work on solids and nets can be found in Book 7.1 Pages 33, 35
> Book 7.2 Pages 31, 34
> Book 7.3 Page 38

34 **Constructions and loci**

LEVEL **7**

KEY FACTS

○ When drawing accurately, you must measure lines to within 1 mm.

○ A locus is the set of all points that fit a given condition or rule. The plural of locus is loci.

○ The locus of a point, which is equidistant from two fixed points A and B, is the perpendicular bisector of the line joining the two points.

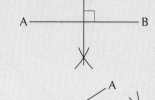

○ The locus of a point, which is equidistant from two fixed lines AB and BC, is the bisector of the angle ABC.

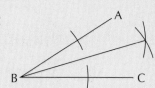

○ Always remember to leave in the construction lines.

Example 1 ▷   Accurately draw a triangle with sides of 5 cm, 6 cm and 8 cm.

Answer 1

Step 1: Draw a base line of 8 cm.

Step 2: Set compasses to 6 cm and draw an arc.

Step 3: Set compasses to 5 cm and draw an arc.

Step 4: Join up the points to complete the triangle.

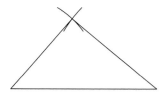

Example 2 ▷   Describe the locus of a point that is always 3 cm from a fixed point **A**.

Answer 2   Set compasses to 3 cm. Draw a circle with its centre at **A**. The locus is a circle of radius 3 cm with its centre at **A**.

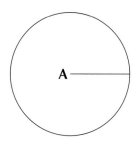

Exercise 34

1 Draw this triangle accurately.

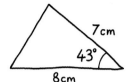

(3 marks)

2 The plan shows the position of three towns A, B and C.

The scale of the plan is 1 cm to 10 km.

A mobile phone mast is to be built.
It needs to be nearer to B than C
and less than 40 km from A.

On a copy of the plan, show the region
where the mast can be built.
Label the region R.

(Remember to leave in your construction lines.)

A •

C •   • B

(3 marks)

3 In this drawing, the shaded area represents a lawn.

A path is to be laid around the lawn so that the edge of the path is always 1 m from the edge of the lawn.

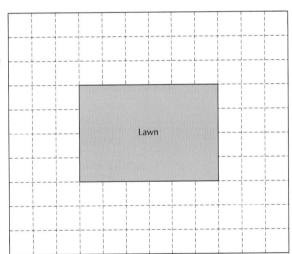

Lawn

Draw a scale drawing to show the position of the path. Use a scale of 1 cm to 1 m.

(2 marks)

4 A goat is tethered by a 3 m length of rope to the corner of a shed that is 1 m by 2 m.

Part of the area that the goat can graze is shown shaded in the diagram.

Draw a scale drawing to show the rest of the area that the goat can graze.

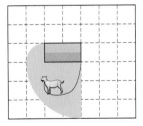

(3 marks)

Further work on loci can be found in Book 9.2 Page 64
Book 9.3 Page 64

KEY FACTS

○ The probability scale goes from 0 to 1:

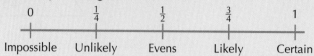

○ Probabilities can be written as fractions, decimals or percentages.

○ To calculate the probability of an event, you need to find all the possible outcomes first and then use the formula:

$$P(\text{Event}) = \frac{\text{Number of outcomes for the event}}{\text{Total number of outcomes}}$$

For example, to find P(Even score), when throwing a dice, there are six equally likely outcomes – 1, 2, 3, 4, 5, 6 – and three of these outcomes are even. So P(Even score) = $\frac{3}{6}$ = $\frac{1}{2}$.

○ When two events occur together, the outcomes can be listed or shown in a sample space table.

For example, when two coins are thrown the four outcomes can be listed as: HH, HT, TH, TT or shown in a sample space table:

	First coin	
	H	T
H	HH	TH
T	HT	TT

Second coin

Example 1 ▷ A bag contains 50 coloured counters. Ten of the counters are red.

A counter is taken out of the bag at random. Which of the values on the right shows the probability that the counter will be red?

$\frac{1}{4}$	10%	0.2
25%	0.1	$\frac{1}{5}$
0.4	$\frac{1}{10}$	20%

Answer 1 There are ten red counters out of a total of 50.
Hence, P(Red) = $\frac{10}{50}$ = $\frac{1}{5}$ = 0.2 = 20%.

Example 2 ▷ A dice and a coin are thrown together.

a Draw a sample space table to show all the possible outcomes.

b Find the probability that the coin lands on heads and the dice lands on an odd number.

Answer 2 **a**

Dice

Coin		1	2	3	4	5	6
	H	1–H	2–H	3–H	4–H	5–H	6–H
	T	1–T	2–T	3–T	4–T	5–T	6–T

b There are three possible outcomes for a head and odd number: 1–H, 3–H and 5–H.
Hence, P(Head and odd) = $\frac{3}{12}$ = $\frac{1}{4}$.

Exercise 35

1 Jamie buys a bag of 20 fruit-flavoured lollipops.

The table shows the number of lollipops for each flavour in the bag.

Flavour	Number
Orange	4
Lemon	6
Strawberry	3
Banana	4
Lime	3

    a Jamie picks a lollipop at random from the pack.

    State whether the following statements are true or false:

      i The probability that he picks a banana-flavoured lollipop is $\frac{1}{4}$.

      ii The probability that he picks either an orange-flavoured or lemon-flavoured lollipop is $\frac{1}{2}$. *(2 marks)*

    b Jamie eats two of the strawberry-flavoured lollipops. He then picks another lollipop at random from the bag.

    What is the probability that he picks a lime-flavoured lollipop? *(1 mark)*

> The probability that I take out a blue disc is $\frac{1}{4}$ because there is 1 blue disc and 4 red discs in the bag.

2 Beth has four red discs and one blue disc in a bag.

She takes a disc out of the bag without looking in the bag.

Explain why Beth is wrong. *(1 mark)*

3 This spinner has five equal sections and five numbers are printed on it.

On the spinner, the probability of scoring a 2 is $\frac{1}{5}$ and the probability of scoring an even number is $\frac{3}{5}$.

What numbers could be on the spinner? *(2 marks)*

4 The following four number cards are placed in a bag.

Marie chooses a card at random, notes its number and then replaces it in the bag.

She takes another card at random and notes its number.

She then adds together the numbers on the two cards she has chosen.

    a Copy and complete the table to show all the possible outcomes.

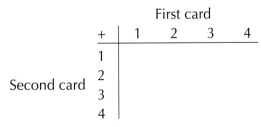

First card

+	1	2	3	4
1				
2				
3				
4				

Second card

(2 marks)

    b What is the probability that her answer is a multiple of 3? *(1 mark)*

    c What is the probability that her answer is greater than 10? *(1 mark)*

Further work on probability can be found in Book 9.1 Pages 128, 131
Book 9.2 Page 129
Book 9.3 Page 150

KEY FACTS

○ If the probability of an event is p, the probability of the event not happening is $1 - p$.

○ If the probability of event A is p and the probability of event B is q, the probability of event A or event B occurring is $p + q$.

○ Relative frequency, or experimental probability, is the number of successful trials divided by the number of trials altogether.

○ The more trials or experiments that are done, the closer the relative frequency gets to the actual (theoretical) probability.

Example 1 ▷

Two fair, six-sided dice are thrown by three students. Their results are shown in the table.

Name	Number of throws	Results		
		No sixes	One 6	Double 6
Alf	20	16	4	0
Beryl	240	164	68	8
Chas	100	65	30	5

a Which student's data is most likely to give the best estimate of the true probability of throwing no sixes, one 6 and double 6? Explain your answer.

b The results are pooled together.

Number of throws	Results		
	No sixes	One 6	Double 6
360	245	102	13

Use the combined results to estimate the probability of throwing:

i No sixes   **ii** One 6   **iii** A double 6 with two dice.

c The theoretical probability of each result is:

P(no sixes) $= \frac{25}{36}$ P(one 6) $= \frac{10}{36}$ P(double 6) $= \frac{1}{36}$

Use these probabilities to work out how many of each result you would expect from 360 throws.

d Explain why the students' results are not the same as the theoretical results.

Answer 1

a Beryl as she has had the most throws.

b **i** $\frac{245}{360}$ or 0.68   **ii** $\frac{102}{360}$ or 0.28   **iii** $\frac{13}{360}$ or 0.04

c 250 with no 6, 100 with one 6 and 10 double sixes.

d The students' results are from a real experiment, so there is an element of chance.

Example 2 ▶

A bag contains only blue, green and red balls. There are 40 balls in the bag altogether. The probability of picking a blue ball at random from the bag is $\frac{2}{5}$.

a What is the probability of taking a ball that is not blue from the bag?

b What is the greatest number of red balls that could be in the bag?

Answer 2

a The probability of a blue ball is $\frac{2}{5}$ so P(not blue) $= 1 - \frac{2}{5} = \frac{3}{5}$.

b There are 16 blue balls ($\frac{2}{5} \times 40$). There must be at least one green ball so the most red balls there could be is 23.

Exercise 36

1 The probability of taking an orange sweet from a bag of sweets is $\frac{1}{8}$.

What is the probability of taking a sweet from the bag that is **not** orange? *(1 mark)*

2 Packets of football cards contain pictures of European footballers.

a The probability of a picture being of a player in the English league is 0.3. Tom buys 40 cards. How many English league players should he expect to have? *(1 mark)*

b Sandra buys some cards and gets 16 pictures of players in the Spanish league. She estimates that the probability of getting a Spanish league player is 0.4. How many cards did she buy? *(2 marks)*

c The makers of the cards claim that the probability of getting a player in the Italian League is 0.2. Eric buys ten cards and gets three Italian league players. Is the manufacturer's claim correct? Explain your answer. *(1 mark)*

3 A group of lower school students have volunteered for a job. The table shows the probability of selecting one of the students at random.

Year	Boy	Girl
Year 7	0.15	0.2
Year 8	0.1	0.25
Year 9	0.05	0.25

a One student is selected at random. What is the probability that the student will be:

i a boy? **ii** **not** in Year 7? *(2 marks)*

b 60 students volunteer altogether. How many of them are Year 7 boys? *(1 mark)*

c The student selected is in Year 9. Is the student more likely to be a boy or a girl? Explain your answer. *(1 mark)*

Further work on probability and relative frequency can be found in Book 9.2 Page 134

Book 9.3 Page 157

37 Surveys and questionnaires

LEVEL 6

KEY FACTS

- When a survey is carried out it should give reliable and unbiased data.
- The sample size should be big enough to give reliable results (at least 30).
- The sample should be representative and not just taken from one type of person or a group of friends.
- The sample should be chosen in such a way that it gives a representative sample, e.g. random sampling, quota sampling.
- Questions on questionnaires should **not**:
  - ask for more than one thing at a time
  - be offensive
  - be worded in a way that forces people to answer in a particular way
  - ask things that might embarrass the person being surveyed.
- Responses on questionnaires should:
  - cover all possible responses
  - give ranges for things like age and income
  - not have any overlapping boxes
  - be kept to a reasonable number (six maximum).

Example 1

A class decides to find out if students in their school would like a new uniform.

a Jasmin says: 'I will ask ten of my friends what they want.'
Give two reasons why Jasmin's method might not produce good data.

b Davos decides to use a questionnaire. This is one of his questions:
The school uniform is very ugly and not very practical. Don't you agree?

☐ Agree a lot   ☐ Agree a little

Give two reasons why Davos' question is not a good one.

c Tamsin says: 'I will send 100 questionnaires around school.'
Which one of the following methods will give the most reliable data?
A: Asking 100 Year 11 students.
B: Asking the first 100 students on the school register.
C: Putting all the names of students in a hat and drawing out 100 names to ask.

Answer 1

a The sample size is too small to give reliable results. Also, asking a group of friends is not likely to give unbiased data as the sample is not representative.

b The question is a leading question as it gives Davos' opinion. It is also badly written as there are two questions in one.

The reponse section only gives options where you have to agree. There is no box to tick if you disagree.

c Method C will give the most reliable data as it is random so gives everyone an equal chance of being picked. Method A would not be representative. Method B may give a good spread of views but is not random.

Exercise 37

1 Some students decide to carry out a survey to find out if people like a new rap artist.

    a One question was: How old are you?

        ☐ 10 or younger   ☐ 10 to 15   ☐ 15 to 20   ☐ Over 20

        Marita said: (The labels for the middle two boxes need changing)

        Explain why Marita is right.   *(1 mark)*

    b Another question was:

        How much do you spend on CDs each month?

        ☐ Nothing   ☐ A bit   ☐ A lot   ☐ Don't know

        Marita said some of the labels also need changing.
        Write new labels for some or all of the boxes.   *(2 marks)*

    c The students decide to survey 100 people.
        Devon decides to ask 100 students in school.

        i   Give one disadvantage of this suggestion.   *(1 mark)*

        ii Give one advantage of this suggestion.   *(1 mark)*

2 These are two questions on Billy's survey on shopping habits.

    Question 1 How much do you spend each week on groceries?

        ☐ £20 or less   ☐ £21 to £30   ☐ £31 to £40   ☐ £41 to £50   ☐ Over £50

    Give one reason why this is a good question.   *(1 mark)*

    Question 2 How many times a week do you buy fruit and/or vegetables?

        ☐ None   ☐ 1 or 2   ☐ 3   ☐ 4 or more   ☐ Every day

    Give one reason why this is not a good question.   *(1 mark)*

3 Karen and Darren want to conduct a survey to find out students' favourite school subjects.

    a Karen decides to survey the 34 students in her Maths class.

        i   Give one disadvantage of Karen's method.   *(1 mark)*

        ii Give one advantage of Karen's method.   *(1 mark)*

    b Darren decides to ask the 15 members of the school football team.
        Give two disadvantages of Darren's method.   *(2 marks)*

Further work on surveys and questionnaires can be found in Book 9.1 Page 176
Book 9.2 Page 183
Book 9.3 Page 212

38 Charts

KEY FACTS

o Charts will usually have a simple scale to read.
o Often the scale is percentage, which will not therefore have actual numbers on.
o Charts are often used to compare two different scenarios.
o Charts will be labelled with a key to help you interpret the information.

Example 1 ▷ The chart on the right shows the ages of police in a country.

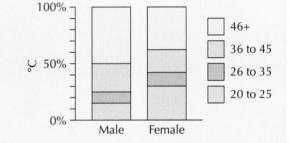

a The chart shows 24% of male police will be aged 36 to 45.

About what percentage of female police will be aged 36 to 45?

b About what percentage of female police will be aged 46+?

c A magazine predicts that there are about 6000 male police aged 46+.

Estimate the number of male police that will be aged between 20 and 25.

d There are about the same number of male police as female police in this country.

Bob says: *Generally the female police will be younger than the male police.*

Bob is correct. Explain how he used the chart to come to this conclusion.

Answer 1 a 20%. The bar can be estimated as two units high. Each unit is 10%.

b The bar is just under four units tall, so the correct answer is about 39%.

c The age group 20 to 25 is about 15% of the force.
The 6000 police aged 46+ represent 50% of the male force, so 100% is 6000 × 2 = 12 000.
To calculate 15% of 12 000 find 10%: 1200 (6000 ÷ 5) and 5%: 600.
So 15% will represent 1200 + 600 = 1800 male police aged 20 to 25.

d The youngest aged bar in the female is almost twice the size of the males and the eldest is much smaller.

Exercise 38

1 Jake and Pike are planning to go on a walking holiday in October. They are trying to choose where to go. They have the following information about the two places they are considering.

Budeo

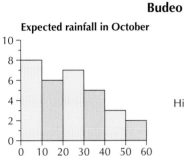

Bernsly

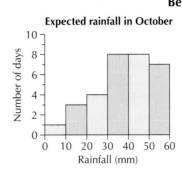

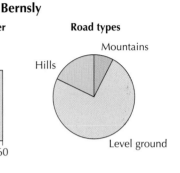

a Which place has the most rain? *(1 mark)*

b Jake and Pike like to walk up hills. Which place has the most hills? *(1 mark)*

c Sam has decided to accompany Jake and Pike on the holiday. She enjoys cycling. Which of the two places would Sam prefer to go to? Fully explain your answer. *(2 marks)*

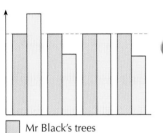

2 Mr Black and Mr Speckle each have four trees. The diagram on the left represents the trees.

a What is the range of the height of Mr Black's trees? *(1 mark)*

b Which person's trees have the greatest mean height? Explain how you know. *(1 mark)*

3 The dual bar chart shows the maximum and minimum temperatures in five cities across Europe in 2005.

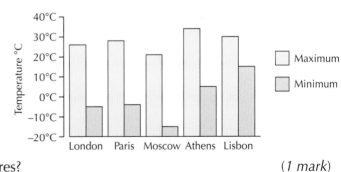

a Which city has the greatest difference between the maximum and minimum temperatures? *(1 mark)*

b Which city has the least difference between the maximum and minimum temperatures? *(1 mark)*

c John says: 'The minimum bar for Athens is about half the size of the maximum bar. This must mean that the minimum temperature is about half of the maximum temperature in Athens.' Explain why John is wrong. *(1 mark)*

d Estimate the difference between the minimum and maximum temperatures in London. *(1 mark)*

Further work on charts can be found in Book 8.1 Page 128
Book 8.2 Page 135
Book 8.3 Page 151

KEY FACTS

o The sectors in a pie chart represent the proportions, not the numbers, so be careful when comparing two pie charts.

o The angles of the sectors in the pie chart all add up to 360°.

o Remember the common percentages in pie charts:
  50% will be a semi-circle sector
  25% will be a quarter of a circle, right-angled sector.

o If asked to sketch a pie chart, do remember to correctly label each sector.

Example 1

The following pie charts show information about the ages of people in two areas of Sheffton. There are 8 thousand people in Grimthorpe, and 2.5 thousand people in Tutly.

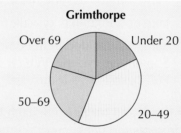
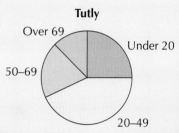

a About what percentage of people in Grimthorpe are aged 50–69?

b Jess says:

> The pie charts show that there are more people under 20 in Tutly than in Grimthorpe.

Jess is wrong.
Explain why the charts do not show this.

c There are about 50 thousand people in Sheffton.

The table shows the approximate percentages of the people in Sheffton in the various age groups.

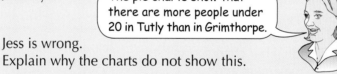

Under 20	20–49	50–69	Over 69
25%	40%	20%	15%

Sketch a pie chart to show the information in the table.

Label each section clearly with the age group.

Answer 1

a 25%. The sector is a right angle, indicating about one quarter of the people in Grimthorpe are in the age group 50–69.

b Because there are more than three times as many people in Grimthorpe than Tutly, the actual number of people under 20 will be much bigger in Grimthorpe.

c
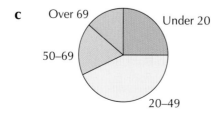

Exercise 39

1 100 members of Avery Youth Club were asked the question: 'Would you play table tennis?'

The pie chart on the right shows their answers.

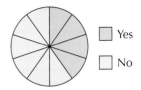

a How many of the youth club members would not play table tennis? *(1 mark)*

b In Banner Cross Youth Club, 50 members were asked the same question.
60% of these members said they would play table tennis.
Which one of the following three pie charts below illustrates this? *(1 mark)*

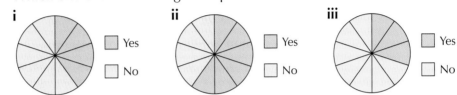

i   Yes   No   **ii**   Yes   No   **iii**   Yes   No

Banner Cross Youth Club
50 members

c How many members of Banner Cross Youth Club said that they would play table tennis? *(1 mark)*

d Emily compares the pie charts and says: 'More members in Banner Cross Youth Club said they would play table tennis than in Avery Youth Club.'
Explain why Emily is wrong. *(1 mark)*

2 Henry paid £540 in council tax one year.
The table shows how the money was spent by the council.
Sketch a pie chart to show the council's spending. *(2 marks)*

Service	Amount
Education	£243
Health	£81
Social Services	£108
Other	£108
Total	£540

3 The following pie chart shows the favourite pets of a number of students.

The angle for 'Cat' is 72°, which represents nine students.

a How many students were surveyed altogether? *(1 mark)*

b 13 students chose 'Dog'. What angle would represent 'Dog'? *(1 mark)*

c In drawing the chart Suzie drew the angle for 'Rabbit' as 90°.
Explain why this is not possible. *(1 mark)*

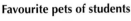
Favourite pets of students

Further work on pie charts can be found in Book 8.1 Page 131
Book 8.2 Page 138
Book 8.3 Page 151

40 Scatter diagrams and lines of best fit

KEY FACTS

- Scatter diagrams show the relationship between two variables.
- The relationship between the variables is called correlation.
- The following diagrams show the main types of correlation.

Strong positive   Weak positive   No correlation   Weak negative   Strong negative

- A line of best fit should be drawn to pass through the middle of the data and be as close to as many points as possible.
- The line of best fit can be used to predict the value of one variable from the value of the other variable.
- When using a line of best fit always draw lines from the axes to show how values were found.
- Lines of best fit do not have to go through the origin.
- Correlation is only valid over the range of the data. Beyond this it is not possible to say if the relationship is valid.

Example 1

Flowers open their petals during the day as they warm up in the sun.

The scatter diagram shows the diameter of the petals at different times of day for a certain flower. The line of best fit is also drawn.

a Estimate the diameter of a flower at 10 AM.

b Estimate by how many centimetres per hour the petals are expanding.

c Explain why you cannot use the scatter diagram to estimate the diameter of the flower at 6 PM.

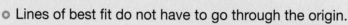

Answer 1

a Draw a line from 10 AM on the Time axis up to the line of best fit, then draw a line across to the vertical axis (dotted on the diagram). This gives a diameter of 2.25 cm.

b At 8 AM the diameter is 1.5 cm and at 2 PM the diameter is 3.5 cm.
So in four hours the increase in diameter is 2 cm. This is 0.5 centimetres per hour.

c The graph only shows the increase from 8 AM to 2 PM. There is no reason to suspect that it continues past this time. In fact, the sun could go in and as it cools down the diameter of the petals will decrease.

Exercise 40

1 The two scatter diagrams below show information about some shops.

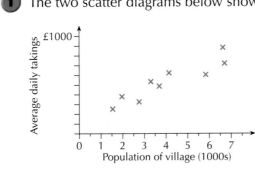
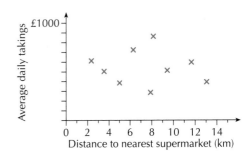

a What does the first graph tell you about the relationship between average daily takings and the population of the village? *(1 mark)*

b What does the second graph tell you about the relationship between average daily takings and the distance to the nearest supermarket? *(1 mark)*

c Draw a line of best fit on the first graph. *(1 mark)*

d A shop opens in a village with a population of 5000 people. What are the expected average daily takings? *(1 mark)*

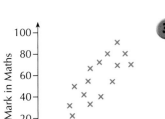
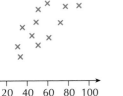

2 The scatter diagram on the left shows the average daily hours of sunshine and the average daily rainfall for ten towns in August.

a Describe the relationship shown by the scatter diagram. *(1 mark)*

b Copy the graph and draw a line of best fit through the data. *(1 mark)*

c Another town has a daily average rainfall of 0.5 cm. Estimate the average daily hours of sunshine for that town. *(1 mark)*

d A third town has a daily average rainfall of 3 cm. Explain why you cannot use the scatter diagram to estimate the average daily hours of sunshine. *(1 mark)*

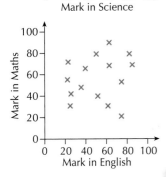

3 The scatter diagrams show the test results of 15 students in English, Maths and Science.

The following scatter diagrams show the results.

a Which of these statements most closely describes the relationship between the scores in the tests. *(2 marks)*

Maths and Science

| Strong negative correlation | Weak negative correlation | No correlation | Weak positive correlation | Strong positive correlation |

Maths and English

| Strong negative correlation | Weak negative correlation | No correlation | Weak positive correlation | Strong positive correlation |

b Which statement most closely describes the relationship between the scores in Science and English. *(1 mark)*

Science and English

| Strong negative correlation | Weak negative correlation | No correlation | Weak positive correlation | Strong positive correlation |

Further work on scatter diagrams and lines of best fit can be found in Book 9.2 Page 74
Book 9.3 Pages 82, 85

41 Mode, mean, median and range

KEY FACTS

○ The mode is the value that occurs most frequently in a given group.

○ The median is the middle value when the data is written in order (or the average of the middle two numbers if there is no middle number).

○ To calculate a mean, sum all the values and then divide by the number of items of data.

○ The range is the difference between the largest and the smallest values.

Example 1 ▷ Find the mode, median, mean and range of the following set of data:

19, 24, 24, 18, 22, 24, 27, 18

Answer 1 Sort the data into order, smallest first: 18, 18, 19, 22, 24, 24, 24, 27

The mode is 24 as this occurs more often than any other number (three times).

To calculate the median, we must take the average of the two middle numbers as there are eight numbers in the set.

Therefore, the median = $\dfrac{22 + 24}{2}$ = 23.

To calculate the mean, add together all the numbers and divide by 8.

Therefore, the median = $\dfrac{18 + 18 + 19 + 22 + 24 + 24 + 24 + 27}{8}$ = 22.

The range of the data is 9 (27 − 18).

Example 2 ▷ Three number cards are turned face down so that the numbers are hidden.

? ? ?

The median of the three numbers is 7 and the range is 5. Two cards are the same.

What could the three numbers be?

Answer 2 The middle number must be 7 as this is the median.

The first and third cards must be different as the numbers have a range of 5 so another card must also be 7 as two cards are the same.

Therefore, the cards must either be 2, 7, 7 or 7, 7, 12.

Exercise 41

1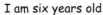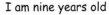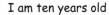

I am five years old   I am six years old   I am nine years old   I am ten years old

    a   What is the median age of the four children?   *(1 mark)*

    b   Which statement about the **median** of their ages in five years time is true?

i It will increase   **ii** It will decrease   **iii** It will stay the same   **iv** It is not possible to tell   *(1 mark)*

    c   Which statement about the **range** of their ages in five years time is true?

i It will increase   **ii** It will decrease   **iii** It will stay the same   **iv** It is not possible to tell   *(1 mark)*

2   **a**   Look at the four cards below. Three expressions are shown. One is hidden.

     $2x + 4$ **?** $2x$ $2x - 3$

     The **mean** value of the expressions is $2x$.
     What is the hidden expression?   *(1 mark)*

    b   What is the mean value of the following two expressions?

     $5x + 3$ $3x - 9$

     Write your expression as simply as possible.   *(2 marks)*

3 In a game three points are awarded for a win, one point for a draw and no points for losing.

    a   Onur played four games. He won one game, drew one and lost the other two.
     What was Onur's mean score over the four games?   *(1 mark)*

    b   George also played four games. His mean score was two points.
Copy and complete the table of results for George.

Number of games won	
Number of games drawn	
Number of games lost	

       (1 mark)

4 This table shows the number of peas in 30 pods.

Number of peas in pod	1	2	3	4	5
Frequency	1	6	9	11	3

    a   Show that the **total** number of peas in the pods is 99.   *(1 mark)*

    b   Explain why the **mean** number of peas is 3.3.   *(1 mark)*

    c   A restaurant serves an average of 35 peas with each meal. They serve 1000 peas on one evening. Approximately how many meals do they serve?   *(2 marks)*

Further work on mode, median, mean and range can be found in Book 9.1 Page 178
Book 9.2 Page 185
Book 9.3 Page 215

42 Discrete and grouped data

KEY FACTS

- Discrete data is data that can take individual values.
- Continuous data is data that can take any value in a range of values.
- Discrete frequency tables are a convenient way of recording large data sets of discrete data where much of the data has the same values.
- Grouped frequency tables are a convenient way of recording large data sets of continuous data by grouping the data together.
- Frequency polygons are used to show the shape of distributions and to compare distributions. The mid-point of the group is plotted against the frequency.

Example 1

Some field mice were caught and weighed in October.

The masses are given to the nearest gram.

The results are shown in the table.

Mass of each mouse (grams)	Frequency f	Mid-point of group m	$m \times f$
16–20	13	18	234
21–25	20	23	
26–30	31		
31–35	17		
36–40	4		

a   How many field mice were weighed altogether?

b   Calculate an estimate of the mean weight of the field mice.
You may complete the table to help you.
Give your answer to 1 decimal place.

c   Field mice with a mass of 22 grams or less will not survive the winter.
Estimate how many of the mice surveyed will not survive the winter.

d   Draw a frequency polygon to show the distribution of masses of the mice.

e   Explain why it is not possible to find the range of the masses of the field mice.

Answer 1

a   85. Add up the total frequency.

b   26.8 (1 dp). The missing mid-points are 28, 33 and 38.
Complete the $m \times f$ column: 460, 868, 561, 152.
The total $m \times f$ is 2275.
The mean is 2275 ÷ 85 = 26.7647.

c   21. There are 20 mice in the group 21–25 so there will be approximately 8 with masses of 21 and 22 grams. Add this to the 13 in the first group.

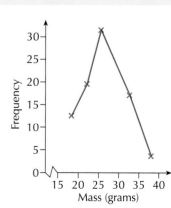

d Plot the frequencies against the mid-points of the group: (18, 13), (23, 20), (28, 31) etc as shown on the previous page.

e There is no indication of the actual masses of the mice, only the group they are in.

Exercise 42

1 Sandra has 12 bags of marbles. The mean number of marbles per bag is 36.

Number of marbles in a bag	34	35	36	37	38
Frequency	3	2	1	4	1

The table shows how many marbles are in 11 of the bags.
Calculate how many marbles are in the twelfth bag. *(3 marks)*

2 A survey was done of birds' nests in a small wood.
61 nests were surveyed and the number of eggs in each was counted.

Number of eggs found in nest	1	2	3	4	5
Frequency	13	23	16	5	4

a Show that the total number of eggs found was 147. *(1 mark)*

b Calculate the mean number of eggs per nest.
Give your answer to 1 decimal place. *(2 marks)*

c It is known that 80% of eggs hatch.
In another large wood there are known to be 526 nests.
Estimate the number of eggs in the large wood that will hatch.
Give your answer to the nearest 10. *(2 marks)*

3 The table shows the heights of 100 tulips grown in a greenhouse.

Height of tulip h (cms)	Frequency f	Mid-point of group m	$m \times f$
$25 < h \leq 30$	11	27.5	302.5
$30 < h \leq 35$	23	32.5	
$35 < h \leq 40$	31		
$40 < h \leq 45$	19		
$45 < h \leq 50$	16		
Total	100		

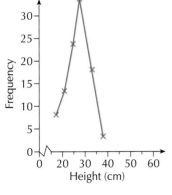

a Calculate an estimate of the mean height of a tulip. Copy and complete the table to help you. *(2 marks)*

b The frequency polygon on the left shows the distribution of the heights of 100 tulips grown outside. On a copy of the same graph, draw the frequency polygon for the heights of the tulips grown in a greenhouse. *(1 mark)*

c Will the mean height of the tulips grown outside be greater or smaller than the mean of the tulips grown in the greenhouse?
Explain your answer. *(1 mark)*

Further work on grouped data and frequency diagrams can be found in Book 9.3 Page 95

43 ## Stem-and-leaf diagrams

LEVEL **6**

KEY FACTS

○ A stem-and-leaf diagram is a way of showing ordered data in a concise way.

○ The stem will normally be the tens digit and the leaves will be the units digit of a number.

○ All stem-and-leaf diagrams should have a key. If you draw one, remember to put a key on it.

○ Always check the key to make sure what values are being represented.

Example 1 ▷ Here is a list of 15 numbers:

23, 31, 28, 42, 37, 33, 31, 26, 31, 29, 41, 30, 34, 25, 38

Put the data into a stem-and-leaf diagram using the key | 2 | 3 represents 23.

Answer 1 First put the data in numerical order from smallest to largest:

23, 25, 26, 28, 29, 30, 31, 31, 31, 33, 34, 37, 38, 41, 42

Now put the data into a stem-and-leaf diagram:

2	3	5	6	8	9			
3	0	1	1	1	3	4	7	8
4	1	2						

Example 2 ▷ The stem-and-leaf diagram below shows students' scores from a Maths test.

Key | 2 | 3 represents a score of 23.

0	9				
1	0	3	5	6	6	8
2	1	3	6	7	
3	6	7			
4	1	2			

a What was the highest test score?

b What is the range of the scores?

c What is the modal test score?

Answer 2 **a** 42 (The largest number is the final value in the table.)

b 33 (The range is the difference between the largest and smallest values, 42 − 9.)

c 16 (The modal test score is the most common value.)

Exercise 43

1 A group of children measured the lengths of some ribbons. Their results were as follows:

18 cm, 42 cm, 33 cm, 22 cm, 30 cm, 25 cm, 47 cm,
54 cm, 35 cm, 38 cm, 26 cm, 32 cm, 42 cm, 48 cm

    a Put the data into a stem-and-leaf diagram using the key
        | 1 | 8 represents 18 cm.   *(2 marks)*

    b How many ribbons did the children measure altogether?   *(1 mark)*

    c What was the length of the longest ribbon?   *(1 mark)*

    d What is the range of the lengths of ribbons?   *(1 mark)*

2 The midday temperature (°C) was recorded in a number of towns on the same day. The results were:

8	14	21	14	3	9	11	17	24
22	18	5	11	4	11	18	23	

    a Draw a stem-and-leaf diagram to represent these data and complete a key.   *(2 marks)*

    b What was the largest temperature recorded?   *(1 mark)*

    c How many towns were included in the survey?   *(1 mark)*

    d What was the range of temperatures recorded?   *(1 mark)*

    e What was the modal temperature recorded?   *(1 mark)*

    f How many towns had a temperature over 20°C?   *(1 mark)*

3 The stem-and-leaf diagram below shows how many driving lessons a number of learner drivers had before they took their driving test.

Key | 2 | 4 represents 24 lessons

```
0 | 9
1 | 3  4  4  7  8
2 | 4  5  5  5  6  8  9
3 | 2  5  8
4 | 6  9
```

    a How many learner drivers took part in the survey?   *(1 mark)*

    b What was the least number of lessons taken?   *(1 mark)*

    c What was the range of the number of lessons taken?   *(1 mark)*

    d What was the modal number of lessons taken?   *(1 mark)*

    e Half of the learners who took less than 20 lessons failed their test. A quarter of the learners who took more than 20 lessons failed their test.

        How many of the learner drivers failed their test?   *(1 mark)*

Further work on stem-and-leaf diagrams can be found in Book 8.1 Page 129
Book 8.2 Page 136
Book 8.3 Page 148

Answers

Exercise 1 Multiplication and division

1 **a** 864 **b** 22230 (1 mark for correct working)
2 **a** 17, remainder 18 **b** 13, remainder 34
3 **a** 432 (1 mark for 18×24) **b** 13 (1 mark for $300 \div 24$)
4 **a** 1855 (1 mark for 53×35) **b** 13 (1 mark for $650 \div 53$)
5 **a** 420 books (1 mark for 35×12)
  b 21 packs (1 mark for $250 \div 12$)
6 **a** £3960 (1 mark for 220×18)
  b 250 (1 mark for $4500 \div 18$)

Exercise 2 Significant figures, approximation

1 **a i** 45 g **ii** 54.999 recurring g **b** 8×45 g = 360 g
2 An explanation saying that some of the seven numbers must have been rounded down. Hence their sum is less than 100.
3 **a** $200 \times 500 \div 20 = 5000$
  b $800 \times 100 \div 2 = 40\,000$
4 **a** 12 **b** 15 **c** 8 **d** Any answer between 10 and 15
5 **a** 4.559924598 **b** 4.6

Exercise 3 Negative numbers

1 **a** −5°C **b** 11°C **c** Bar from −16° C to −4° C
2 **a** −3, −15 **b** −10, −4
3 **a** Any valid values e.g. -2×-10, -1×-20, -4×-5
  b Any valid values e.g. $-4 - -24$, $-8 - -28$,
4 **a** 4, −3 (1 mark for any two values with a product of −12, 1 mark for any two values which add together to make 1)
  b −2, −6 (1 mark for any two numbers with a product of 12, 1 mark for any two numbers which add together to make −8)
  c −6
5 **a** −2 **b** −15 **c** −8 **d** −16 **e** + 8 **f** −10

Exercise 4 Fractions

1 **a** £16.50 **b** £12 **c** $\frac{5}{8}$ **d** £12
2 240 90 $\frac{1}{2}$ $\frac{3}{4}$
3 **a** 0 $\frac{1}{4}$ $\frac{1}{2}$ $\frac{7}{12}$ $\frac{2}{3}$ 1 **b** 1, 16, 5
4 **a** 12 **b** 4 (1 mark if $\frac{12}{5} \times \frac{5}{3}$ seen)
5 **a** $1\frac{1}{3}$ cm² (1 mark for $\frac{1}{2} \times \frac{4}{5} \times \frac{10}{3}$, 1 mark for units)
  b 30 (1 mark if method seen $40 \div \frac{4}{3}$)
6 **a** $\frac{11}{20}$ **b** $4\frac{1}{24}$ **c** $1\frac{1}{2}$ **d** $1\frac{1}{3}$
7 **a** $\frac{3}{16}$ **b** $\frac{7}{12}$
8 $\frac{2}{7}, \frac{5}{16}, \frac{1}{3}, \frac{3}{8}$ (1 mark for finding common denominator)

Exercise 5 Decimals

1 **a** 67.2 **b** 25.6 **c** 5.43 **d** 0.904
2 **a** 10 **b** 0.824 **c** 100 **d** 4.89
3 **a** 6.04 **b** 33.35 **c** 4.24 **d** 5.64
4 **a** 21.35 **b** 32.67 **c** 16.5 **d** 4.63
5 **a** 35.2 **b** 352
6 $£22 + £12 + £8 = £42$ (deduct 1 mark for each error in the table)
7 **a** 69.4 km **b** 21.8 km
8 £78.21 (1 mark for £26.25 and 1 mark for £51.96)
9 £72.80
10 One fifth of £48 (1 mark for £9.60 or £9.25)

Exercise 6 Percentages

1 **a** £10.50 **b** 75% **c** £35
2 **a** North America **b** 60.7 or 61% (1 mark for $3737 \div 6157 \times 100$)
3 **a** 17.5% **b** 116 the 115.3 need to be rounded up (1 mark for $17.5 \div 659 \times 100$)

Exercise 7 Percentage and proportional change

1 **a** 25 **b** 30
2 **a** 24.3 miles (1 mark for 6.3) **b** 22.2% (1 mark for digits 222)
3 **a** $4.59 **b** £17.50 **c** 434 (1 mark for $558 \div 180 \times 140$)
4 **a** £64 (1 mark if $40 \times 160/100$ or equivalent seen)
  b 2 weeks – 1 month (1 mark for $44.2 \div 68$)
5 **a** £216 (1 mark for $15 \times 1440/100$)
  b 12% (1 mark for $1282 \div 10682$)
6 **a** 0.14×56 **b** 1.56×14 **c** 1.15
7 29.5% (1 mark for $162925 \div 552479$ (= 0.2948...))

Exercise 8 Ratio

1 **a** 1 : 3 **b** 3 : 5 **c** 2 : 7 **d** 3 : 4
2 **a** 1 : 3.5 **b** 1 : 2.5 **c** 1 : 1.6 **d** 1 : 2.7
3 750 g (1 mark if 250 seen)
4 **a** 7 : 8 **b** 12
5 **a** £16 and £64 (1 mark if 16 seen)
  b 36 kg and 84 kg (1 mark if 12 seen)
6 9 squares shaded on the diagram (1 mark for showing $24 \div 8$)
7 100 oak trees, 200 beech trees and 300 sycamore trees (1 mark for showing $600 \div 6$)
8 **a** Hannah £24 and Jack £36 (1 mark for showing $60 \div 10$)
  b Hannah £25 and Jack £35 (1 mark for showing $60 \div 12$)
9 1 : 2 (1 mark for black area = 12 and 1 mark for grey area = 24)
10 **a** 3 : 5 **b** 5 : 8
  c The large tin (1 mark for showing, for small tin, 1p for 9.6 g. 1 mark for showing, for large tin, 1p for 10 g)

Exercise 9 Powers and roots

1 **a** 128 **b** 729 **c** 100 000 000
2 **a** 4^8 **b** 5^6 **c** 7^{12}
3 **a** $x = \pm 4$ (1 mark for 4) **b** $x = \pm 10$ (1 mark for 10)
  c $x = \pm 3$ (1 mark for 3)
4 **a** $x = 4$ **b** $x = 3$ **c** $x = 2$
5 **a** $3^4 = 81$ (1 mark for 3 correct from 32, 81, 64, 25, 6)
  b 4^3
6 **a** $a = 2, b = 4$ **b** $m = 3, n = 2$
7 **a** $2n$ **b** $\frac{1}{n}, n^2$ and $\sqrt{n}$ (1 mark for 2 correct)
  c $\frac{1}{n}, \frac{n}{2}$ and $\sqrt{n}$ (1 mark for 2 correct)
8 0 and 1
9 **a** 6 and 7 **b** 9 and 10 **c** 14 and 15
10 6.5 cm
11 4.6 m
12 **a** For example: $\sqrt{9} \times \sqrt{16} = \sqrt{144} = 12$ (1 mark for substituting 2 different numbers)
  b For example: $\sqrt{9} + \sqrt{16} = 7 \neq \sqrt{25}$ (1 mark for substituting 2 different numbers)

Exercise 10 Number patterns and generalisation

1 **a** Column 3 **b** 46 **c** $5n - 2$ **d** Row 7
2 **a** 10001 **b** $n^2 + 1$ **c** 29
3 $H = 5M + 1$
4 **a i** $n^2 - n + 1 + 1 = n^2 - n$ **ii** $n^2 - n + 1 - 1 = n^2 - n$
  b $12^2 - 12 + 1 = 144 - 12 + 1 = 133$
  c n^2

Exercise 11 Expressions, formulae and equations

1 b, e, f
2 c, d
3 **a i** $7a + 6$ **ii** $3b + 7$ **b i** $5b + 3$ **ii** $3a + 4$
4 **i** The perimeter is 12 cm **ii** Side PQ is 3 times as long
  as PM **iii** Side PM is 2 cm less than side MQ

Exercise 12 Functions and inverse operations

1 $x \to \dfrac{x + 2}{3}$
2 **a** 77°F **b** 15°C
3 7
4 **a** £16.20 **b** $27 \div 0.9$

Exercise 13 Solving linear equations

1 **a** The number of red and green pencils is 11.
  b The number of blue pencils is three times the number of red
  pencils.
  c There are 17 more blue pencils than green pencils.
2 **a** $p = 2$ **b** $m = 3$ **c** $y = 6$ (1 mark for $2y = 12$)
  d $x = -\frac{1}{2}$ (1 mark for $2x = -1$)
3 $x = 4.5$ (1 mark), length = 20.5 cm, width = 2 cm
4 $x = 3$ (1 mark for $x + 10 + x - 4 = 4x$)
5 **a** $3x - 7 = 23$, $x = 10$ **b** 11

Exercise 14 Algebraic expressions

1 $3x + 5$ $x - 1$ $x - 3$ $2x + 1$ $6(x + 3)$ or $6x + 18$ $12x + 4$
2 **a** $5x - 1$ **b** $3x + 4$ **c** $x + 5, y + 5, x + y + 10$
  d $2x + 1, 4x + 3, 4x + 2$
3 **a** $8x - 2$ (1 mark for $4x - 1$)
  b $3x - 1, 2x + 3$
4 **a** $9a - 2$ **b** $6a + 2$ **c** $8a - 5$

Exercise 15 Expansion of brackets

1 **a** $a^2 + 9a + 18$ (1 mark for two correct terms)
  b $b^2 - 3b - 4$ (1 mark for two correct terms)
  c $c^2 + c - 42$ (1 mark for two correct terms)
  d $d^2 - 9d + 20$ (1 mark for two correct terms)
  e $e^2 - 4e + 4$ (1 mark for two correct terms)
  f $15 - 2f - f^2$ (1 mark for two correct terms)
2 **a** $(x + 4)(x + 6)$ **b** $y^2 - 11y + 18$ (1 mark for two correct terms)
3 $A = \frac{1}{2}(p + 10)(p + 6) = \frac{1}{2}(p^2 + 16p + 60) = \frac{1}{2}p^2 + 8p + 30$
  (1 mark for correct expansion)
4 **a** n^2 cm², $3n$ cm², $6n$ cm², 18 cm² (1 mark for two correct terms)
  b $n^2 + 9n + 18$
5 It should be $x^2 + 10x + 25$ (1 mark for two correct terms)
6 **a** $(x + y)(x - y) = x^2 - xy + xy - y^2 = x^2 - y^2$ (1 mark for correct
  expansion)
  b i 35 **ii** 800 **iii** 1200

Exercise 16 Factorising

1 $2a^2b^2$ and $18ab$
2 **a** $3(4a + 20) = 2(6a + 30)$ **b** $5(4b - 1)$
3 $3y^2(y - 6)$ as it is equivalent to $3y^3 - 18y^2$. All the others are
  equivalent to $3y^3 - 9y^2$.

4 **a** $4(x + 3)$ **b** $5x^2(2x - 1)$
5 Both Alan and Beth are right as the two expressions are
  equivalent.
6 Let integers be n, $n + 1$, $n + 2$
  $n + n + 1 + n + 2 = 3n + 3 = 3(n + 1)$, which is a multiple of 3
  (1 mark for $3n + 3$)
7 **a** $4n + 6$ **b** $2(2n + 3)$
  c $4n + 6 = 2(2n + 3)$, which is a multiple of 2, therefore even.

Exercise 17 Substitution

1 **a** 41 **b** 14 **c** 11.25
2 **a** 14 **b** 2 **c** 0.56
3 **a** 32°F **b** 212°F **c** 98.8°F (1dp) **d** 17.6°F
4 **a** 16.5p (accept 17p) (1 mark for $330 \div 20$)
  b $2\frac{1}{2}$ minutes (1 mark for showing $180 = t + 30$)
5 **a** £52.50 (1 mark for $25.5 + 27$) **b** 4 (1 mark for showing
  $35 = 17 + 4.5c$)
6 **a** 55 **b** 1275 **c** 500 500
7 **a** 18.4 m/s (1 mark for showing $100 + 240$)
  b 37.9 m/s (1 mark for showing $1600 - 160$)

Exercise 18 Proof and explanation

1 **a** False, it is always even: $3(3 + 1) = 12$, $2(2 + 1) = 6$
  b True, at least one of the numbers must be even:
  $3(3 + 1)(3 + 2) = 60$
  c True, if n is even, $n^2 + 1$ is odd; if n is odd $n^2 + 1$ is even:
  $2^2 + 1 = 5$, $3^2 + 1 = 10$
2 **a** When x is odd x^2 is odd because odd × odd = odd.
  b When x is odd $(x - 1)(x + 1)$ is even as both brackets are even
  and even × even = even.
3 Calculation is approximately $\dfrac{40 \times 55}{30 - 10} = \dfrac{2200}{20} \approx 110$ so the
  answer is 'Right'. (2 marks for 110, 1 mark for $2200 \div 20$)
4 **a** Any value of x which is greater than 0 but less than 1.
  b $x = 0$ or 1 **c** Any value of x less than 0 or greater than 1.
5 **a** 1080°. An octagon can be split into six triangles.
  $6 \times 180 = 1080°$
  b The statement is true because the polygon splits into two
  fewer triangles than the number of sides (1 mark) and the
  angle sum of each triangle is 180° (1 mark).
6 **a** It is not possible to make a triangle because the two smaller
  sticks, when put together, are still shorter than the longest stick.
  b Assume the equal sides are 1, then the sides are 1, 1, 11
  which won't make a triangle.
  This is also the case with 2, 2, 9 and 3, 3, 7. But if the equal
  sides are 4 or 5 then the triangle is 4, 4, 5 or 5, 5, 3, and 6,
  6, 1, all of which obey all three rules.

Exercise 19 Graphs from real life

1 **a** 80 metres **b** 40 metres **c** The smallest distance in
  good weather is 80 m, in bad it is 120 m. You must increase
  the space by 40 metres.
2 **i** 68 **ii** 28 **iii** 68 **iv** 80 **v** 12
  These measurements can be higher or lower by 1 (1 mark for
  3 correct, 2 marks for 4 correct, 3 marks for 5 correct)
3 **a** Paul **b** 400 m **c** George in 5 minutes **d** $\frac{1}{2}$ minute

Exercise 20 Graphs of linear equations

1 **a** Yes, because $2 \times 20 + 1 = 41$ **b** (2.5, 6)
  c $y = 2x + c$, where c is any value except 1
2 **a**

Number of people	0	10	20	30
Total cost of admission	0	£51	£102	£153

b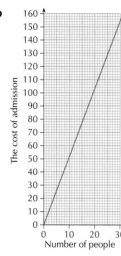

(1 mark for plotting points)

c £127.50 (allow £127–£128)

3 **a** A: $x = 1$, B: $y = x + 1$, C: $y = 6$, D: $x + y = 4$
b A and B, because $y = 2x$ also has the coordinates (1, 2)

Exercise 21 Solving inequalities

1 **a** $-1 < x < 2$ **b** $-1 \leq x \leq 4$ **c** 0 or 1
2 **a** $x = 3$ **b** $x > 3$ **c** $x < -3$
3

	$x + y > 4$	$x + y < 4$
$y > x$	A	B
$y < x$	D	C

4 **a** $-6 \leq n \leq 6$ **b** $-10 < n < 10$
5 **a** $n \geq 3$ or $n \leq -3$ **b** $n > 5$ or $n < -5$
6 **a** $x > 18$ **b** $x \leq 2$ **c** $x > -1$

Exercise 22 Triangles and quadrilaterals

1 **a** Drawing of a trapezium
b Drawing of an isosceles right-angled triangle
2 **a** Yes, two sides are equal and the base is shorter.
b Yes, opposite sides are parallel and equal in length.
c No, adjacent sides are different lengths.
3 **a**   **b**

4 **a** In an equilateral triangle every angle is 60° and all the sides are equal.
b In a rectangle every angle is 90° and opposite sides are equal.

Exercise 23 Angles in a polygon

1 $a = 180 - 75 = 105°$ $b = 180 - 25 = 155°$ $c = 180 - 80 = 100°$
2 $x = 180 - 85 = 95°$ $y = (360 - (3 \times 85)) \div 3 = 35°$
3 Each angle in an equilateral triangle is 60°, hence $a = 60°$
$b = 180 - 60 = 120°$
4 **a** $(4 - 2) \times 180 = 360°$ **b** $(6 - 2) \times 180 = 720°$
5 **a** Any of *PBA, PAB, ARD*   **b** Any of *DAB, ADR*
c $180 - 75 - 65 = 40°$
6 **a** $((5 - 2) \times 180) \div 5 = 108°$ **b** $108 - 90 = 18°$
c $(180 - 108) \div 2 = 36°$

Exercise 24 Pythagoras' theorem

1 9.8 km (2 marks for 9.76***, where *** can be anything),
(1 mark for 95.29)
2 12.49 cm (1 mark for $16^2 - 10^2$ or 156)
3 11.31 cm (2 marks for 11.31***, where *** can be anything),
(1 mark for 128)

4 $5^2 + 12^2 = 25 + 144 = 169$, $13^2 = 169$, hence $5^2 + 12^2 = 13^2$,
so a right-angled triangle (1 mark for 169)
5 325 m (1 mark for 105 300)

Exercise 25 Circumference and area of a circle

1 30.85 cm (1 mark for 18.85 cm)
2 **a** 113.1 cm   **b** 8840 times (1 mark for 1 000 000 cm)
3 Yes, with full justification, e.g. Circumference is 785.4,
785.4 ÷ 75 > 10. (2 marks for 785.4 ÷ 75, 1 mark for 785.4)
4 157.1 cm² (1 mark for 314.2 cm²)
5 6.8 cm² (2 marks for $\pi \times 1.9^2 - \pi \times 1.2^2$, 1 mark for either
$\pi \times 1.9^2$ or $\pi \times 1.2^2$)
6 **a** 81.7 cm   **b** 6.9 cm (1 mark for 47.7)
7 5.6 cm (2 marks for 2.8 cm, 1 mark for 25 ÷ π)
8 4.5 cm (1 mark for 28 ÷ 2π)
9 64% (2 marks for 200 ÷ 314.2 × 100, 1 mark for 314.2)

Exercise 26 Area of plane shapes

1 **a** Any rectangle with an area of 6 cm², e.g. length 3 cm,
width 2 cm
b Any rectangle with an area of 10 cm², e.g. length 5 cm,
width 2 cm
c Any rectangle with an area of 8 cm², e.g. length 2 cm,
width 4 cm
d Any rectangle with an area of 20 cm², e.g. length 5 cm,
width 4 cm
2 A (area of rectangle and parallelogram = 12 cm², triangle = 6 cm²)
3 Any triangle with an area of 6 cm², e.g. triangle base = 6 cm,
height = 2 cm
4 Shapes B, C and D

Exercise 27 Volume of 3-D shapes

1

3	2	4
3	1	8
2	2	6
4	1	6

2 **a** 48 cm³ (1 mark if units not stated)   **b** $x = 8$
3 **a** 750 m³ (1 mark for showing area of trapezium = 75 m²)
b 750 000 litres
4 320 cm³ (1 mark for showing cross-sectional area is 40 cm²)
5 385 cm³ (1 mark for showing the calculation: $\pi \times 3.5^2 \times 10$)

Exercise 28 Units of measurement

1 **a i** pounds   **ii** grams   **b i** litres   **ii** pints
2 Yes, she is right. The weights of the seven people total 502 kg.
Multiplying this by 2.2 gives 1104 pounds, which is more than
the maximum permitted weight. (1 mark for 502 × 2.2, 2 marks
for 1104 pounds)
3 **a** 4 × 1000 = 4000 g   **b** 1.2 × 1000 = 1200 ml
c 1.08 × 1000 = 1080 kg
4 **a** 9.1 m (30 × 12 × 2.54 ÷ 100 = 9.144)
b 197 ft (60 × 100 ÷ 2.54 ÷ 12 = 196.85) (1 mark for correct
working)
5 25 miles per hour (1 mark for 5 m ≈ 8 km)

Exercise 29 Compound measures

1 1.6 m/s (1 mark for showing 125 s)
2 40 km/h (1 mark for finding time = 2.5 hours)
3 6 litres (1 mark for showing 90 km)
4 **a** 6 km/h   **b** 30 minutes   **c** 4 km/h

5 **a** 40 mph **b** 52 mph **c** 48 mph

6 3 hours 20 minutes (1 mark for showing 200)

Exercise 30 Transformations

1 **a** and **c** Check diagram

b 90°

2

(1 mark for each correct vertex)

3 $a = 4$, $b = 5$ and $c = 120$

4 (in each case deduct a mark for every error)

a enlargement, 2, (4, 4) **b** rotation, clockwise, 90, (1, 4)

c 3, 2, down **d** reflection, $y = -1$

Exercise 31 Parallel lines

1 **a** 60° **b** 50° **c** 70°

2 **a** $3x$ **b** $4x = 180$ **c** $x = 45°$

3 The angle vertically opposite 115° is also 115°. This angle and angle x are allied angles, so they add up to 180°. Hence, $x = 180 - 115 = 65°$. (1 mark for $x = 65°$ with no explanation)

4 **a** The transversal will be perpendicular to the parallel lines.

b The transversal will cut the parallel lines at an angle of 45°.

5 **a** 70° **b** 45° (1 mark if 135° shown in working)

Exercise 32 Isometric drawings

(In all questions, give 1 mark if 2 dimensions correct)

1 **2** **3.**

4 **5**

Exercise 33 Solids and nets

1

This shows one possible net, there are other possible answers.

2 **a** 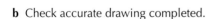 **b** Check accurate drawing completed.

3

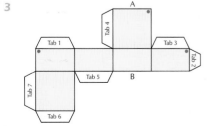

Exercise 34 Constructions and loci

1 Accurate drawing with lines within 1 mm and angle within 1 degree

2

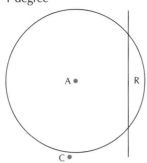

(1 mark for correct perpendicular bisector of BC with construction lines)

(1 mark for circle with radius 4 cm, centred on A)

(1 mark for correct position of R)

3

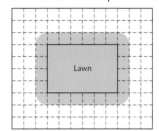

Lawn

(1 mark for four correct straight lines shown)

(1 mark for four correct arcs from vertices shown)

4

(1 mark for part of circle radius 1 m, 1 mark for $\frac{3}{4}$ circle radius 3 m and 1 mark for $\frac{1}{4}$ circle radius 2 m)

Exercise 35 Probability

1 **a** **i** False **ii** True **b** $\frac{3}{18}$ or $\frac{1}{6}$

2 The correct answer is $\frac{1}{5}$ because there are five discs in the bag and only one is blue.

3 The five numbers are 2, any two even numbers other than 2 and any two odd numbers (1 mark for three correct numbers)

4 **a**

		First card		
+	1	2	3	4
1	2	3	4	5
Second card 2	3	4	5	6
3	4	5	6	7
4	5	6	7	8

(1 mark for two correct columns or rows)

b $\frac{5}{16}$ **c** 0

Exercise 36 Relative frequency

1 $\frac{7}{8}$

2 **a** 12 **b** 40 (1 mark for $16 \div 0.4$) **c** Possibly as P(Italian) = 0.3, but the sample is too small to be sure.

3 **a** **i** 0.3 **ii** 0.65 **b** 9 **c** A girl as there are five times as many girls as boys

Exercise 37 Surveys and questionnaires

1 **a** She is right because there are overlapping boxes. For example, a 10-year-old could tick two boxes.

b Any reasonable labels that do not overlap. For example:

☐ £0 ☐ £0.01–£4.99 ☐ £5.00–£9.99 ☐ £10 or over

c i They will only get a sample from people aged 11 to 16 so it will not be representative.

ii It will be easy to organise and the sample size is good.

2 Question 1 is good because it is relevant to the survey, responses cover all values and there are no overlapping responses.

Question 2 is bad because there are two questions in one about fruit and vegetables and there are overlapping responses.

3 a i The sample may not be representative.

ii It will be easy to organise and the sample size is big enough.

b The sample is too small.

The sample is not representative: they will probably pick sport as the favourite subject.

Exercise 38 Charts

1 a Bernsly

b Budeo

c You can have either place provided you have given a clear reason, eg Bernsly because there is more level ground there, or Budeo because there will be less rain to cycle in.

2 a 0

b Mr Black's. You can see that the total height of Mr Speckle's trees will be less since he has two much smaller trees and only one higher by a similar amount.

3 a Moscow **b** Lisbon **c** The bars do not start at zero.

d 27–32°C

Exercise 39 Pie charts

1 a 60 **b** ii **c** 60% of 50 = 30 members

d Because in Avery YC 40% of 100 would play table tennis, which is 40 members. This is larger than the 30 at Banner Cross YC.

2 45% of the money is spent on education, 15% on health, 20% on social services and 20% on other. Angles in a pie chart total 360° so you should therefore have a pie chart with angles of 162° for education, 54° for health, and 72° each for social services and other. They should all be labelled. (1 mark if angles correct but incorrectly labelled)

3 a 72° is 20% of 360°. Therefore 20% of the students surveyed liked cats. 9 students liked cats so the total number of people surveyed is 9 × 5 = 45.

b 104°

c Does not divide by 8°, which is the angle per student.

Exercise 40 Scatter diagrams and lines of best fit

1 a Average daily takings increase with the size of the village (positive correlation).

b There is no relationship between daily takings and distance to nearest supermarket.

c
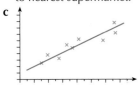

d £580–£620

2 a As the hours of sunshine increases, the rainfall decreases (negative correlation).

b
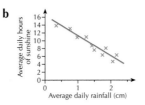

c 13 hours

d The graph is only valid up to 2 cm of rainfall.

3 a Maths and Science, weak positive correlation
Maths and English, no correlation

b Science and English, no correlation

Exercise 41 Mode, mean, median and range

1 a 7.5 years **b i** It will increase **c iii** It will stay the same

2 a $2x - 1$ **b** $4x - 3$ (1 mark for $8x - 6$)

3 a 1 point

b

Number of games won	2
Number of games drawn	2
Number of games lost	0

4 a $1 \times 1 + 2 \times 6 + 3 \times 9 + 4 \times 11 + 5 \times 3 = 2 + 10 + 27 + 44 + 15 = 99$

b 99 peas ÷ 30 pods = 3.3 peas per pod

c 28, 29 or 30 (1 mark for 1000 peas ÷ 35 = 28.57 meals)

Exercise 42 Discrete and grouped data

1 38 (1 mark for total marbles = 12 x 36 = 432, 1 mark for total in 11 bags = 394)

2 a $1 \times 13 + 2 \times 23 + 3 \times 16 + 4 \times 5 + 5 \times 4 = 147$

b 2.4 (1 mark for 147 ÷ 61)

c 1010 (1 mark for 526 × 2.4 × 0.8)

3 a 37.8 cm (1 mark for total of 3780)

b See right
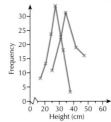

c Smaller as the frequency polygon for the outside plants is to the left of the frequency polygon for the inside plants.

Exercise 43 Stem-and-leaf diagrams

1 a

```
1 | 8
2 | 2  5  6
3 | 0  2  3  5  8
4 | 2  2  7  8
5 | 4
```

(1 mark for the correct stem; 1 mark for the correct leaves)

b 14 **c** 54 cm **d** 36 cm

2 a

```
0 | 3  4  5  8  9
1 | 1  1  1  4  4  7  8  8
2 | 1  2  3  4
```

Key: | 1 | 3 represents 13° C
(1 mark for the correct diagram; 1 mark for the correct key)

b 24°C **c** 17 **d** 21°C **e** 11°C **f** 4

3 a 18 **b** 9 **c** 40 **d** 25 **e** 6